Single Parent's Guide to Everything

By
K.F. Anthony

©2024 by Care Collective Firm

All rights reserved. No part of this publication may be reproduced, distributed, or transmitted in any form or by any means, including photocopying, recording, or other electronic or mechanical methods, without the prior written permission of the publisher, except in the case of brief quotations embodied in critical reviews and certain other noncommercial uses permitted by copyright law.

For permissions requests, write to the publisher at the address below:

Care Collective Firm

Austin, Texas

Contact@CareCollectiveFirm.com

CareCollectiveFirm.com

This guide is provided for informational purposes only. The author and publisher make no representations or warranties with respect to the accuracy or completeness of the contents of this guide and specifically disclaim all warranties, including without limitation, warranties of fitness for a particular purpose.

The advice and strategies contained herein may not be suitable for every situation. Consult with a professional where appropriate. Neither the author nor the publisher shall be liable for any loss of profit or any other commercial damages, including but not limited to special, incidental, consequential, or other damages.

Trademarked names may appear throughout this guide. Rather than use a trademark symbol with every occurrence, we are using the names only in an editorial fashion and to the benefit of the trademark owner, with no intention of infringement of the trademark.

Printed in United States of America

ISBN for print: 978-0-9995889-1-8

ISBN for ebook: 978-0-9995889-0-1

Contents

Introduction	1
Chapter 1: Caring Solo: Single Parenting Wisdom and Co-Parenting Resources	4
Chapter 2: Resilient Radiance: Self-Care and Health for Single Moms and Dads	27
Chapter 3: Dollars and Sense: Smart Money Management for Single Parents	46
Chapter 4: Learning and Earning: A Single Parent's Guide to Education and Career	54
Chapter 5: Business/Entrepreneurship for Single Parents	59
Chapter 6: Navigating Unleashing Potential: Single Parenthood and Disability	67
Chapter 7: Empowering Resilience: Navigating Single Parenthood Through Domestic Challenges	77
Chapter 8: Navigating New Beginnings: Divorce, Dating, and Building a Support Network	83
Acknowledgement	103
References	104

Introduction

Being a single parent is hard! I know, because I've been there. While there are many resources out there to help you, it can be overwhelming to find the right ones. This book is designed to serve as your guide to everything—from finding a shelter if you're homeless to maintaining good mental health while providing for your children.

The fact that you are reading this book indicates that you are looking for more information, resources, and support to help you in your role as a single parent.

Embarking on this book is my way of letting you know that, as a single parent, you're not alone in your journey. Today, there's an abundance of information, resources, and support available to help you navigate the unique challenges you may encounter.

If you're reading this, it means you're seeking more insights, resources, and support for your role as a single parent. Each chapter is a guide, delving into topics such as connecting with single parents facing similar situations, carving out precious time for yourself, mastering budgeting and saving, addressing school bullying, and finding the help you might need.

Within each chapter, you'll discover a wealth of resources, providing avenues for additional information. From expert advice on solo parenting to practical how-to videos, websites featured in the book offer a spectrum of guidance.

Moreover, there are links to groups specializing in diverse needs, from housing and transportation to legal advice. This book covers it all – connecting with fellow single parents, finding time for self-care, managing finances, addressing school challenges, and seeking help when needed. It's a comprehensive resource tailored to the solo parent journey, with each chapter crafted to empower and support you.

Someone who has been there has written each page of this book.

I understand the challenges of being a single parent due to divorce, as I've personally walked that path myself. The journey can be tough, and the weight of the situation can feel overwhelming. Yet, by sharing my experiences and offering guidance on navigating the uncertainties that arise, this book aims to instill hope for a brighter future for you and your children.

Remember, you're not alone in this journey. Many others have confronted challenges similar to yours and discovered solutions that can also benefit you. Allow this book to serve as a source of support and encouragement as you navigate the unique landscape of single parenthood.

Discover within each chapter of the Single Parent's Guide to Everything a carefully curated selection of online resources, recommended reads, insightful articles, and handy tools. Supplemental downloads are also available to enhance your understanding and provide valuable support on your journey as a single parent.

If you're seeking support groups, keep an eye out for upcoming chapters where I'll share suggestions to connect you with valuable communities ready to provide assistance. Your journey as a single parent is supported by a wealth of information and connections outlined in the chapters ahead.

You are not alone in this journey!

Consider this book as a companion, guiding you through the daily challenges encountered by single parents. It's not an exhaustive manual, but rather a starting point—a supportive guide for your unique journey. It's crucial to gently remind yourself that you're not alone; others are confronting challenges and uncovering useful ways to overcome them. The key is to success is to keep pressing forward, never losing sight of your potential or the bright future awaiting you and your children.

As we delve into the intricacies of our lives as single parents, the more we learn, the better equipped we become to face whatever lies ahead for us and our families. Let this guide be a source of encouragement and insights as you navigate your path.

This guide is designed with both new single parents finding their footing and seasoned single parents seeking additional support in mind. Whether you're just beginning your journey into this new chapter of life or aiming to expand your toolkit of resources and support services, my hope is that it offers valuable assistance on your path towards a better and brighter future.

Chapter 1

Caring Solo: Single Parenting Wisdom and Co-Parenting Resources

Delve into the realms of parenting and co-parenting with this chapter. Explore the intricacies of these roles and discover valuable insights on how to navigate them effectively as a single parent. From understanding the essence of co-parenting to seeking ways to encourage positive involvement from your ex, this chapter serves as a guide for a balanced and harmonious approach to parenting in the context of single parenthood.

Parenting As A Single Parent

Navigating parenthood comes with its own set of decisions and responsibilities. As a single parent, balancing these aspects can be challenging, especially when managing everything on your own. That's where this guide steps in! To support you on this journey, here are some tips and resources designed to assist you in providing the best for your children and helping them flourish into successful adults.

Understand that you're a wonderful parent.

You are truly an exceptional parent. Juggling the responsibilities of single parenthood is no easy feat, yet you handle it with grace and resilience. It's natural to have moments of self-doubt, but know that you're not alone in this journey.

Your dedication to your children is truly commendable, and they look up to you as a role model. As they grow, they will reflect the same selflessness and kindness that you embody, becoming extraordinary individuals who love unconditionally—just like their remarkable parents.

Take care of yourself - for your own well-being and for the sake of your children.

As a single parent, prioritizing self-care is crucial. When you feel good, you're better equipped to be the best parent you can be. Ensuring you're well-rested, eating healthily, and getting enough sleep can provide the energy and patience needed for your children. Taking time for yourself is equally important, allowing you to relax and savor moments with your kids.

Don't hesitate to seek support from family and friends when facing stressors like school schedules or financial issues. Engaging with other parents in the community can provide valuable insights into what has worked for them in similar situations. Remember, you don't have to navigate these challenges alone; there are resources and a supportive community ready to assist.

Allow your kids to have their feelings about the situation.

When children are involved, divorce or a separation is never an easy situation to navigate. Your child may experience feelings of guilt or sadness as the family undergoes this change. They might harbor anger or resentment towards one of the parents and find it challenging to comprehend why this path was chosen. Understanding that both parents are good people who made mistakes may be difficult for them. The fundamental shift in their family structure can also be unsettling, leading to worries about what's happening at home and potential sleep difficulties due to anxiety about the future.

It's crucial to create a space where your kids feel comfortable expressing their emotions, even if their words are painful for you to hear. If you carry any shame about the situation (a perfectly normal sentiment), try not to project those feelings onto your children. Instead, encourage them to openly share their feelings without judgment, irrespective of their age or societal expectations.

Equally important is to listen attentively without imposing your own emotions or attempting to invalidate theirs. Assure them that it's okay to feel sad or angry; they are not obligated to be happy about the situation just because it aligns with others' expectations. Let them know that their feelings are valid and deserving of acknowledgment.

Be flexible and open to how things work out, instead of trying to control the situation.

Embrace flexibility and openness in how things unfold, rather than striving to control every aspect of the situation. Be receptive to change and unafraid to explore new approaches.

Release concerns about external opinions or judgments. Your status as a single parent is inconsequential—what truly matters is that you are doing the best job possible, providing your children with everything they need in every conceivable way. Avoid unnecessary guilt for aspects beyond your control or decisions you feel could have been different; it's not a burden worth carrying.

Be tolerant of the challenges and difficultly that parenting is likely to bring.

Acknowledging that being a single parent can be challenging is the first step toward moving forward. Understand that you'll experience both good and tough days—parenting, by its nature, has its difficult moments.

Avoid the trap of comparing yourself to other parents or setting unrealistic expectations. If you ever feel overwhelmed to the point of contemplating giving up or believe someone else could provide better care for your child, consider taking a break and seeking support from an outside group where individuals facing similar situations can offer valuable insights and help navigate challenges together.

Remind yourself that certain events, like illness or injury, may be beyond your control. Try not to blame yourself or carry unnecessary guilt; life unfolds in unexpected ways. Moreover, resist the urge to place excessive pressure on yourself; having children doesn't mean the rest of your life should come to a standstill—they can coexist harmoniously.

Have good support and ask for help whenever you need it.

Engage with your children's school counselors to gain insights into their experiences and collaborate on a plan for addressing any challenges they may be facing.

Connect with a support group, either through online forums or physical gatherings, where you can share your thoughts and experiences with others navigating similar situations.

Consider involving a therapist, recognizing that therapy is beneficial for children as well. Your child may require additional support in processing their emotions about the divorce or separation, especially if their behavior indicates underlying distress. Acting out is a common response, but if it persists or worsens over time, therapy can equip them with new coping skills and emotional resilience.

Don't hesitate to seek assistance from family and friends, particularly those who have gone through similar experiences. If you find it challenging to secure help with daily tasks like preparing dinner or managing laundry, remember that your needs matter too. Don't let others disregard your feelings; seek individuals who genuinely care about your well-being and the challenges you face as a single parent.

Stay positive and focus on the positives that being a single parent brings.

Maintain a positive outlook and concentrate on the strengths that come with being a single parent.

While the challenges of single parenthood can be daunting, there are numerous ways to make it more manageable. One effective approach is to shift your focus from dwelling on the negatives to highlighting the positives of being a single parent. If you find yourself overwhelmed with responsibilities and lacking a support system, take a moment to reflect on the positive aspects. Challenge yourself to jot down at least five positive things each day for a week. This process sets the stage for the next step: celebrating and honoring those qualities within yourself.

Your children will thrive when you create and maintain a balance of self-care and parenthood

Allocate time for yourself as a parent:

To be an effective parent, prioritizing your well-being is essential. If you're consistently stressed and fatigued, connecting with and caring for your children can become challenging. Allow yourself moments to relax, reflect, and regroup, enabling you to approach parenting decisions with a calm state of mind.

Establish clear boundaries:

It's perfectly acceptable if others disagree with how you choose to spend your time. However, it's crucial to uphold the understanding that this is YOUR life, and there are times when YOUR needs must take precedence. Don't hesitate to decline requests that demand too much of your time or energy—it's not selfish; it's a vital aspect of self-preservation!

Single parents encounter diverse challenges, yet it's essential to acknowledge your ability to navigate this journey successfully. You can create a stable and loving home for your children. Stay true to yourself and grounded in the present as you navigate the challenges of single parenthood, prioritizing what's best for your children. Remember you're never alone on this journey and there are abundant resources available to provide extra support whenever you need it. My trusty guide is here to lend a helping hand along the way.

Here are some of my favorite nationwide parenting resources for single parents:

1. Single Parent Support Groups: Explore local and online support groups for advice, encouragement, and shared experiences among single parents.
2. Single Parenting Websites: Websites like SinglePar-ent.com, SingleParentMeet.com, and SingleParentsNetwork.com offer tailored articles, forums, and resources.
3. National Single Parent Helpline: Access helplines like the 24/7 Single Parent Helpline (1-800-4-A-CHILD) for free counseling and support.
4. Government Assistance Programs: Check government websites for programs like SNAP, TANF, and Medicaid supporting single parents.
5. Local Community Centers: Many community centers offer parenting classes, workshops, and resources designed for single parents.
6. YMCA/YWCA: Organizations like YMCA and YWCA often provide family programs, childcare, and support services.
7. Nonprofit Organizations: Groups like Single Parent Advocate and Parents Without Partners offer resources, events, and advocacy.
8. Online Parenting Forums: Platforms like Reddit, BabyCenter, and CafeMom host active single parenting communities.
9. Parenting Books: Find inspiration and advice in books like "The Successful Single Parent" by Honoree Corder and "Single Parents by Choice" by Jane Mattes.

10. Local Churches and Religious Organizations: Seek support, counseling, and community from religious institutions.

11. Parenting Workshops and Webinars: Stay informed about local workshops and online webinars on parenting topics.

12. Childcare Resources: Research affordable childcare options, including daycare centers, afterschool programs, and babysitting services.

13. Online Parenting Blogs: Follow blogs like "Single Mommyhood" and "The Single Swan" for personal stories and resources.

14. Therapists and Counselors: Consider seeking professional help through therapy directories specializing in single parenting.

15. Legal Aid Services: Explore resources like Legal Aid organizations for assistance with legal matters.

16. National Parent Helplines: Access helplines like the Parent Helpline (1-855-4A-PARENT) for advice and support.

17. Online Parenting Courses: Platforms like Coursera and Udemy offer a variety of online parenting courses.

18. Parenting Podcasts: Tune in to podcasts like "The Single Mom Podcast" and "Parenting Solo" for insights and tips.

19. Financial Assistance Resources: Explore options such as FAFSA and scholarship programs for single parents pursuing higher education.

20. Employment Resources: Find flexible job opportunities on websites like FlexJobs and Mom Corps.

21. Mentorship Programs: Seek programs like Big Brothers Big Sisters for positive role models for your children.
22. Parenting Magazines: Magazines like "Single Parent Magazine" and "Single Parent Advocate Magazine" offer relevant articles.
23. Online Workshops and Webinars: Participate in online workshops covering co-parenting and stress management.
24. Parenting Apps: Use apps like "Cozi" for organizing family schedules and "JustParents" for connecting with other single parents.
25. Legal Resources: Websites like FindLaw and LegalZoom provide information and resources for legal matters.
26. Health and Wellness Resources: Explore organizations offering healthcare information, mental health support, and wellness tips.
27. Parenting Social Media Groups: Connect with others on platforms like Facebook and LinkedIn in various parenting groups.
28. National Childcare Associations: Organizations like NAFCC can provide information on quality childcare options.
29. Financial Planning Resources: Find guidance on budgeting, saving, and financial planning for single parents.
30. Volunteer Organizations: Platforms like VolunteerMatch help you find volunteer opportunities for giving back while connecting with others.

Single parents are often overwhelmed and looking for ways to connect with other single parents and get relevant help.

Single parents often feel overwhelmed, searching for connections and relevant assistance. Numerous parenting resources designed for single parents are accessible both online and offline, many of which are budget-friendly or free. You can explore more about these resources to aid you in your parenting journey. The best way to discover such resources is by looking for them in your local area. Utilize search engines like Google, entering "parenting resources" followed by the name of your city or town to find options near you.

There are many parenting resources available specifically for single parents online and offline.

Single parents often feel overwhelmed, searching for connections and relevant assistance. Numerous parenting resources designed for single parents are accessible both online and offline, many of which are budget-friendly or free. You can explore more about these resources to aid you in your parenting journey. The best way to discover such resources is by looking for them in your local area. Utilize search engines like Google, entering "parenting resources" followed by the name of your city or town to find options near you.

Countless parenting resources cater to single parents, with both online and offline options. Offline facilitators are available to assist single parents in navigating the challenges they may encounter. It's crucial to acknowledge that it's okay not to have all the answers and that you don't have to navigate parenthood alone.

Co-parenting

There are many kinds of co-parenting situations for single parents, and each one has its own challenges. Single parents can experience various types of co-parenting situations, including:

1. Inseparable Co-parents:
- Involves one mom and one dad navigating co-parenting responsibilities together.
2. Separate but Equal Co-parents:
- Involves two moms or two dads sharing co-parenting responsibilities independently.
3. Two Households with Shared Parenting Schedules:
- Parents maintain separate households while sharing parenting schedules.
4. Joint Custody:
- Involves one or both parents having primary custody, with shared parenting schedules.

The type of co-parenting situation you are in can influence the approach to your divorce process.

If you're a single parent who hasn't been involved in co-parenting before, you might feel overwhelmed with all the new things you have to think and talk about.

For single parents new to co-parenting, navigating the myriad of responsibilities can be overwhelming. Learning effective communication with your co-parent is key. Here are some tips for managing these new dynamics:

- Schedule Regular Meetings:
- Stay connected with your co-parent by scheduling regular meetings. Opt for in-person or phone discussions rather than relying solely on emails.
- Flexibility in Co-parenting Schedule:
- Remain flexible with your co-parenting schedule. Rigidity can lead to conflicts or resentment.
- Open and Honest Communication:
- Be open and honest with your co-parent, especially during disagreements. Assume good intentions and strive to understand each other's perspectives.
- Flexibility in Parenting Styles:
- Embrace flexibility in parenting styles. Avoid being overly rigid, as it can lead to conflicts.
- Non-Judgmental Approach:
- Refrain from judging each other's parenting styles. Acknowledge that everyone is doing their best for the well-being of their children.

If you need help managing complicated co-parenting dynamics, consider talking to a therapist who specializes in relationships, or joining a group support group for single parents.

If you find it challenging to collaborate with your co-parent, seeking the guidance of a therapist specializing in relationships can be beneficial. A therapist can help you navigate your feelings and those of your co-parent by asking insightful questions and exploring the underlying issues. They may also propose strategies to address conflicts.

If individual therapy is not feasible, joining a support group for single parents can offer valuable insights. These groups provide a platform for individuals to share experiences, seek advice, and find solace in dealing with challenges unique to single parenting or co-parenting situations.

You may want to get help managing your divorce or custody issues by hiring an attorney or working with a mediator.

Seeking assistance in managing divorce or custody matters is advisable, whether through hiring an attorney or engaging a mediator. In some cases, reaching an agreement on parenting arrangements without going to court can be in the child's best interests. For instance, if both parents agree on holiday arrangements for the children, it can be considered sufficient for the time being.

A mediator, distinct from a judge, facilitates an agreement between parents concerning parenting arrangements and financial matters. Mediators assist parents in gaining clarity about their situation, understanding each other's perspectives, and collaboratively devising solutions, empowering them to make decisions without external imposition.

Managing schedules can be one of the most challenging aspects of co-parenting because it involves managing two households on top of work commitments.

Coordinating schedules in co-parenting can be a significant challenge, particularly when juggling two households and work commitments. To alleviate this, we recommend starting by proactively dividing your child's holidays and birthdays in advance. This approach minimizes the time spent figuring out schedules, ensuring everyone gets quality time with their children.

For effective co-parenting, it's crucial for single parents to promptly communicate any scheduling changes or conflicts to ensure inclusivity. If, for instance, a parent experiences an unexpected work schedule change, immediate communication allows the partner to adjust plans accordingly. Similarly, resolving conflicting plans, such as choosing a venue for the kids' birthday party, in advance can prevent last-minute surprises and potential conflicts during event planning.

Communication

Setting up a communication strategy with your co-parent is an important part of co-parenting and will make things run more smoothly when crisis strikes.

As you work on setting up communication with your co-parent, it will be helpful to discuss how often and what tools you want to use. Some options include:

- Face-to-face meetings (in person or via video)
- Texting
- Phone calls

Effective communication with a co-parent is essential for fostering a healthy environment for your children. Begin by setting a positive tone, focusing on the needs and well-being of the child. Keep conversations brief and to the point, reducing the likelihood of misunderstandings. Choose the right communication method based on the situation – whether it's in-person discussions, phone calls, or written messages. Be open to listening, acknowledging each other's perspectives, and finding common ground. Establish clear boundaries and guidelines, respecting each other's schedules and commitments. Utilize tools like shared calendars and apps designed for co-parenting communication to enhance organization and reduce conflicts. Always maintain a cooperative attitude, prioritizing the best interests of your children throughout the co-parenting journey.

Co-parenting can be difficult, but there are tools you can use to make it easier for yourself and your family.

In co-parenting, staying organized is key. Utilize a calendar or shared folder to track your children's schedules, ensuring everyone is on the same page. Effective communication is vital for maintaining open lines between you and your co-parent, despite challenges such as time zones, distance, and differing schedules. These factors can complicate relationships, but implementing sound communication strategies can help overcome these obstacles.

Staying organized as a co-parent is essential for effective communication and smooth coordination. Here's a guide to help you stay organized:

1. Shared Calendar:

- Use a shared online calendar to keep track of your children's schedules, including school events, extracurricular activities, and visitation plans.
- Color-code entries for each parent to provide a quick visual reference.

2. Communication Platform:

- Choose a dedicated platform for co-parenting communication. This could be a shared document, a messaging app, or a co-parenting-specific app.
- Keep all relevant information, discussions, and updates in one accessible location.

3. Document Sharing:

- Establish a system for sharing important documents, such as school reports, medical records, and legal documents.
- Cloud storage platforms or shared folders can facilitate easy access for both parents.

4. Regular Check-Ins:

- Schedule regular check-ins to discuss upcoming events, changes in schedules, or any concerns.
- Consistent communication helps prevent misunderstandings and ensures everyone is on the same page.

5. Emergency Information:

- Keep an updated list of emergency contacts, medical information, and essential details in a shared document or accessible location.
- Share this information with relevant parties, such as caregivers or school personnel.

6. Respectful Communication:

- Practice clear and respectful communication. Clearly express expectations, and be open to compromise when necessary.

- Avoid using communication platforms for personal disputes; instead, focus on co-parenting matters.

7. Flexibility and Adaptability:

- Embrace flexibility and be adaptable to changes in schedules or unforeseen circumstances.
- Communicate promptly about any modifications to the agreed-upon plan.

8. Parenting App Utilization:

- Explore co-parenting apps designed to streamline communication and organization. These often include features like shared calendars, expense tracking, and messaging.

9. Consistent Routine:

- Establish a consistent routine for exchanging children and stick to agreed-upon schedules as much as possible.
- Predictability can reduce stress for both parents and children.

10. Professional Guidance:

- If needed, consider involving a mediator, counselor, or family therapist to facilitate communication and provide guidance on co-parenting strategies.

Remember, the key to successful co-parenting organization is clear communication, mutual respect, and a commitment to working together for the well-being of your children.

Difficult Conversations

Co-parenting with a challenging ex-spouse can be demanding, but focusing on effective strategies can help navigate this situation.

Maintaining clear and concise communication, using neutral platforms or co-parenting apps, and strictly adhering to the court-ordered parenting plan can establish a more structured and less contentious co-parenting arrangement. Seeking professional support, such as mediation or counseling, is beneficial for resolving conflicts and fostering better communication.

Prioritizing the well-being of your children, controlling emotional responses, and considering a parallel parenting approach can contribute to a more stable co-parenting dynamic. Documenting interactions and seeking legal advice when necessary are essential steps to address challenges within the framework of the court order.

Ultimately, the key is to remain patient, prioritize self-care, and commit to the best interests of your children, creating a healthier co-parenting environment despite the difficulties with your ex-spouse.

Helpful Resources

Learning how to co-parent effectively is a skill that can be acquired, improved, and mastered over time. With the right tools and techniques, anyone can become proficient in the art of co-parenting. Several organizations provide excellent resources to support your journey in effective co-parenting:

1. National Families in Action
2. National Family Law Center
3. The Parent Education Network
4. Co-Parenting.com
5. National Parents Organization
6. National Alliance for Shared Parenting Incorporated

The National Divorce Support Forum

The National Divorce Support Forum, facilitated by the American Academy of Matrimonial Lawyers, serves as a valuable resource for individuals navigating divorce. Comprising lawyers, mediators, financial advisors, and mental health professionals, this forum provides free support and offers paid services such as workshops and one-on-one counseling sessions.

Exploring dedicated sections on stepfamilies and divorce specifics, the National Divorce Support Forum offers insights into co-parenting challenges, especially when dealing with remarriage or new relationships. If you're encountering difficulties in co-parenting, this forum can be a helpful starting point to understand best practices and state-specific guidelines

Explore the resources offered by these organizations to enhance your co-parenting skills and navigate the journey successfully.

Your local library

Your local library serves as an excellent resource for co-parenting information. Offering books, online resources, educational videos, and articles, libraries contribute to your understanding of co-parenting. Look out for workshops or classes on co-parenting, potentially hosted at your children's school or community center. Your local librarian might also organize support groups in your area, providing additional assistance and guidance.

Co-parenting Books to Read

Explore a vast selection of co-parenting, divorce, stepfamilies, and co-parenting books on Amazon.com and Barnes & Noble (BN.com). Whether searching by title or author, you'll find a diverse range of books to cater to your specific needs and preferences.

Discover insightful books on co-parenting through popular titles such as "It's Not Complicated" by Alysha Price, "Co-Parenting with a Toxic Ex" by Amy J.L. Baker and Paul R. Fine, "Mom's House, Dad's House: Making Two Homes for Your Child" by Isolina Ricci, and "The Co-Parenting Handbook: Raising Well-Adjusted and Resilient Kids from Little Ones to Young Adults through Divorce or Separation" by Karen Bonnell. These resources offer valuable guidance for navigating the complexities of co-parenting and fostering positive relationships with your child.

I hope this chapter has given you some helpful information about the process of co-parenting, and how to make it work for you. If you're a single parent who hasn't been involved in co-parenting before and feel overwhelmed by all the new things you have to think and talk about, consider talking to a therapist who specializes in relationships or joining group support group for single parents. You may want to get help managing your divorce or custody issues by hiring an attorney or working with a mediator.

Additional co-parenting resources:

Our Family Wizard: An online platform designed to help divorced or separated parents communicate, share schedules, and manage expenses in a cooperative manner.

CoParenter: An app that focuses on facilitating communication and organization between co-parenting, including features like shared calendars and expense tracking.

Up To Parents: An evidence-based program offering online tools and resources to help parents develop effective co-parenting skills and minimize conflict.

Kids' Turn: An organization that provides workshops and resources to help parents and children cope with the challenges of divorce and separation.

Online Support Groups: Websites like Daily Strength and Smart Co-parent offer online support communities where co-parents can share experiences, advice, and encouragement.

Family Mediation Services: Mediation services can help co-parents resolve disputes and reach agreements outside of court, promoting more cooperative co-parenting relationships.

National Parents Organization: An advocacy group that aims to promote shared parenting and fair custody arrangements, offering resources and support for co-parents.

Family Court Support Services: Look for local resources provided by family court systems, which may include co-parenting classes, workshops, and mediation services.

Therapists and Counselors: Seeking professional therapy or counseling can provide co-parents with valuable tools for effective communication and conflict resolution.

Parenting Plan Templates: Websites like CustodyXChange offer templates for creating comprehensive parenting plans that outline schedules, responsibilities, and guidelines for co-parents.

Parenting Classes: Many community centers and organizations offer parenting classes that cover co-parenting strategies and communication skills.

Cooperative Parenting Institutes: These institutes offer workshops and resources to help parents develop the skills necessary for successful co-parenting.

Local Family Support Organizations: Look for local nonprofit organizations focused on family support, as they may offer co-parenting resources, workshops, and counseling.

Legal Aid and Mediation Centers: Seek out legal aid centers and mediation services that can provide guidance on legal matters related to co-parenting.

Parenting Blogs and Books: Follow blogs like "Co-Parenting 101" by Deesha Philyaw and Michael D. Thomas, and "The Co-Parenting Handbook" by Karen Bonnell for expert advice and insights.

There are many resources available to help you learn how to co-parent effectively.

Unveiling the art of co-parenting resembles acquiring any skill – it involves learning, improvement, and mastery. Regardless of your previous experience, these tools and techniques empower anyone to navigate co-parenting successfully. Here are organizations providing excellent resources for effective co-parenting:

- National Families in Action
- National Family Law Center
- The Parent Education Network
- Co-Parenting.com
- National Parents Organization
- National Alliance for Shared Parenting Incorporated

In conclusion, co-parenting is a demanding yet vital aspect of ensuring the well-being of your children. With the resources highlighted in this guide, you now have valuable tools and insights to navigate this journey successfully. Remember, making co-parenting work effectively is achievable with the right support, allowing you to foster a positive environment for your family and children. We trust these resources will be beneficial. For further inquiries or additional support, please explore www.singlemomssociety.com.

CHAPTER 2

Resilient Radiance: Self-Care and Health for Single Moms and Dads

I understand the challenges of being a single parent and the overwhelming love you have for your children. Balancing parenting responsibilities can be exhausting, making self-care seem like a distant luxury. However, integrating self-care into your life is possible without turning your home into chaos. Let's explore manageable ways to prioritize self-care amidst the demanding journey of single parenthood.

Self-care is important for everyone, but it's especially important for single parents.

Self-care, simply put, involves activities or practices that enhance your well-being and satisfaction with life. It ranges from indulging in a soothing bath to immersing yourself in nature or engaging in meaningful conversations with friends or family. Self-care is not a luxury but a fundamental need for everyone, especially for those navigating the challenges of single parenthood. Studies have highlighted that individuals practicing self-care are more likely to experience happiness. This isn't just about personal joy; it directly influences your ability to provide the attention and care your children deserve. Amidst the demanding responsibilities of solo parenting, prioritizing self-care becomes crucial for sustained well-being and effective parenting.

Self-care makes you feel better and helps you recharge.

Self-care holds particular significance for single parents as you are your sole support system, responsible for meeting your own needs. The more you invest in your well-being, the greater reservoir of energy you'll have available for your children. Single parents often bear the weight of multiple roles, being expected to fulfill diverse responsibilities. This multifaceted role can be time-consuming and draining, potentially leading to feelings of resentment if the load isn't shared. Prioritizing self-care is not a luxury but a necessity to prevent burnout, ensuring you can navigate your myriad responsibilities without compromising your own health and happiness. It's a vital investment in maintaining balance and resilience amid the demands of solo

Self-care can help you be more patient with your kids.

Self-care is not just for single parents, but it can be especially important to take time for yourself. As a single parent, you are often concerned about your children's health and happiness—and rightly so! But sometimes, the stress of taking care of everyone else can lead you to neglect your own needs. If you don't take care of yourself, how will you be able to provide the love and attention that your children need? They look up to you as an example; they want what is best for them just like any child would. When we feel good about our lives (or at least less stressed out), we're more likely to have patience with our kids—and that makes us better parents!

Self-care doesn't need to be expensive to be meaningful.

Self-care doesn't need to be expensive or time-consuming. You don't have to go on an expensive vacation, sign up for a yoga retreat, or buy a bunch of fancy stuff. Self-care can be as simple as taking a walk with the kids through your neighborhood, sitting down and reading a book for pleasure instead of reading about work, and getting out into nature whenever possible (even if it's just a few minutes in the backyard).

Your self-care can also involve spending time with friends or family members and doing activities together that you all enjoy—and it doesn't matter if those activities cost money! It can even be something like sitting down and having lunch with friends at work instead of eating alone at your desk (which is actually another form of self-care). If you're feeling stressed out by being a single parent, take some time now to think about things that make you feel good—and then go do them!

There are lots of self-care options for single parents, even if you have little time and money.

1. Take a walk or go for a run.
2. Enjoy a relaxing bath for self-care.
3. Play with your kids, showing them you're taking time for yourself.
4. Read a book in the tub to enhance relaxation.
5. Explore self-care and single parenthood books, whether from the library or online.
6. Utilize libraries as a free resource for various books, including memoirs and expert insights.

Here are a few more self-care options for single parents.

Journaling Tips For Single Parents

Journaling serves as a powerful tool to externalize your thoughts, liberating them from the chaotic confines of your mind. This practice aids in processing emotions and navigating overwhelming situations. Additionally, journaling facilitates self-awareness by highlighting the existence of feelings, their physical manifestations, and the insights they provide about oneself. The versatility of journaling allows for various approaches, such as freeform writing, numbered lists, bullet points, poetry, prose, or even expressive doodles. Choosing the method that resonates with you enhances the effectiveness of this introspective practice. Beyond personal clarity, writing thoughts down contributes to organizing them coherently, aiding in effective communication with others.

Try a Personal Development Book Club

Engaging in personal development through reading can significantly contribute to your self-care routine. While time constraints might limit your reading, joining a book club provides a structured opportunity to indulge in regular reading. Beyond the literary benefits, book clubs offer a social dimension, enabling you to build connections and friendships. Surrounding yourself with individuals invested in your well-being enhances your mental health and fosters a supportive network.

Enjoy Simple Pleasures

Make your commute more enjoyable by listening to music or an engaging audiobook. Whether it's a lively bus ride or a carpool with fellow parents, this can transform a hectic morning into a more relaxing experience. When the weather is pleasant, take advantage of your lunch break outdoors. Find a serene spot at a local park, beach, or picnic table to soak up the sunshine, feel the breeze, and savor the fresh air. Use this time to reconnect with old friends who live nearby and make the most of your surroundings.

Tap Into Audio

Enhance your daily commute by tuning in to music or an engaging audiobook. Whether navigating a bustling bus ride or sharing a carpool with fellow parents, these moments can become more relaxed and enjoyable. Embrace the soothing tunes or captivating stories as you traverse from school drop-off to work, or take a leisurely stroll through town, a parking lot, or a mall, immersing yourself in your personal soundtrack through headphones.

Go Outside

Embrace the warm weather by having your lunch outdoors. Seek out a pleasant spot at a local park, beach, or picnic table—anywhere that allows you to relish the sunshine, feel the breeze, and breathe in fresh air. Use this time to reconnect with old friends who reside nearby, turning your lunch break into a delightful moment of relaxation and socializing.

Pamper Yourself with an At Home Spa Day

A self-care day at home is a great way to feel good and relax. Here's how:

Use essential oils. These can be used in many ways, such as putting them in the bath or adding them to your skin after showering. If you do this, make sure that you follow the recommended usage amounts, which are usually on the bottle or box.

Have someone give you a hot stone massage (or do it for yourself). While massaging is great for helping with muscle aches and pains, having someone else do it for you can also be relaxing because it helps relieve stress from your life as well as giving time and attention to yourself (which is important). If no one else will massage you (or if they have other things going on), consider buying some therapeutic stones that can go into warm water so they heat up before using them on your back or neck area while watching TV!

Do facial masks at home with ingredients found in most kitchens like banana peels mixed with honey or yogurt mixed with cucumber slices pressed into an overripe avocado half—you get creative here! Mix two tablespoons each of baking soda and water together until smooth then apply directly onto face after removing makeup/cleanse face first."

Try Getting In Some Exercise

Incorporating exercise into your routine as a single parent can be challenging, but it's crucial for your well-being. While it might be difficult to commit to an hour-long gym session every day, there are numerous ways to stay active without leaving your home.

Consider getting a gym membership if you prefer a more structured environment. Alternatively, take short walks around your neighborhood to rejuvenate and boost your energy. Gradually increase the duration of these walks over time, turning them into a simple yet effective way to stay active.

Taking a break from the constant demands of parenting is crucial for single parents. If affordable, hiring a babysitter or nanny can provide the freedom to step away without worrying about your children's safety. This respite allows you guilt-free time to focus on yourself. These moments of self-care contribute to relaxation and well-being, nurturing your ability to navigate the challenges of single motherhood effectively.

As a parent, prioritizing self-care is crucial. Why not give some of these ideas a try today and invest in your well-being?

In conclusion, prioritizing self-care as a single parent is not only beneficial but also essential for your health and well-being. Despite the challenges and busy schedules, finding time for sufficient sleep and regular exercise is crucial, not just for your physical health but also for your emotional balance. These tips aim to guide you in incorporating self-care into your routine, ensuring you maintain a healthy and balanced life as a dedicated parent.

Health and Single Parents

Navigating the challenges of being a single parent is no easy feat. Balancing the roles of a parent, caregiver, and individual responsible for your own health can be overwhelming. However, there are actionable steps you can take to prioritize your well-being while also ensuring the health of your children. In this chapter, we'll explore strategies for single parents to focus on their health, promoting a sustainable and healthy future for both themselves and their kids.

Having health insurance is vital.

Maintaining health insurance is crucial for covering healthcare expenses, managing chronic conditions, and accessing preventive and mental health care—especially significant for any single parent.

Make your doctor's appointments a top priority.

Make your doctor's appointments a top priority. Don't make excuses for not going, even if it means taking time off work or finding childcare for the kids. Your health is too important to put off until later.

Make sure everyone in the family gets regular check-ups, including immunizations if needed. If you don't have health insurance through an employer or through Medicare/Medicaid/CHIP/etc., call their customer service line (on their website) and ask them what steps will be necessary for getting coverage once again after leaving another plan.

Consider buying an individual policy if you don't have a job that offers coverage.

Ensure that everyone in the family receives regular check-ups, including necessary immunizations. If you lack health insurance through an employer or programs like Medicare/Medicaid/CHIP, visit their website's customer service line and inquire about the required steps for reinstating coverage after leaving another plan

Find low-cost or free clinics in your area for annual checkups and other health needs.

A free clinic offers healthcare, medications, and various services without charge, catering to individuals without insurance coverage or financial means. Typically funded by charitable donations, government grants, and on-site fees (like lab test costs), these clinics may provide payment plans to make medical bills more manageable. To locate a nearby free clinic, you can check the directory of Federally Qualified Health Centers (FQHCs) on HealthCare.gov: [FQHC Directory](). If an option closer than your current provider's office is available but poses scheduling challenges, discussing remote consultations with your doctor through video chat platforms like Skype might be worth considering, although planning ahead is necessary. Keep in mind that this option may have privacy and security considerations.

Look into discounted dental coverage, even if it isn't offered through your employer.

Save on dental care costs by exploring comprehensive plans beyond the basics, even if not provided by your employer. Inquire with your employer about discounted dental plans, especially relevant if your children are still covered by parental insurance. Contact your state's dental association for insights on dentists offering discounts or income-based programs aiding bill payments. Check local hospitals, organizations, and churches for discounted plans, and explore eligibility for Medicaid assistance programs. It's worth reaching out to Medicaid to inquire about available low-cost services and assistance programs, considering their specific limitations on qualifying treatments.

Look into federal, state and local programs that provide free or low-cost services to qualifying family members.

Explore federal, state, and local programs providing free or low-cost services for eligible families. Medicaid, a joint federal-state program, offers health insurance coverage for low-income individuals and families, with eligibility varying by state and dependent on income, household size, and disability status. Check your state's Medicaid office for details on eligibility requirements and potential dental benefits.

Single parents must manage their own care while also ensuring their kids are getting proper healthcare.

Prioritize self-care as a single parent by scheduling regular checkups, avoiding unhealthy habits like smoking and excessive drinking, and dedicating time to activities you enjoy. Maintaining your well-being contributes to positive interactions with others, fostering a happier environment for yourself and those around you. Single parents, facing the dual responsibility of self and children, benefit from self-care practices, promoting a healthy and joyful life for the entire family.

Conclusion

As you can see, there are a lot of things to consider when it comes to taking care of yourself and your family. It's important that you take time each day for yourself, even if it's just five minutes of quiet meditation or deep breathing. And don't forget about exercise! Regular physical activity will help boost your mood and keep you healthy. If you're having trouble getting started with an exercise routine, try joining a gym with childcare services so that other parents can help keep an eye on their kids while also getting in some workouts themselves. Good luck!

Wellness for Single Parents

Embarking on my solo parenting journey, I underestimated the significance of wellness. My children played a pivotal role in making me recognize that self-care is essential for me to be the best mom I can be. As a single parent, prioritizing wellness becomes even more crucial, particularly when serving as the primary caregiver for your children.

Parents have a lot on their plates.

Balancing work, kids' activities, housework, and errands as a single mom can make self-care seem elusive. However, prioritizing yourself is vital for your health and wellbeing. It not only ensures your strength for your family but also empowers you to give your best to them.

What is wellness?

Wellness is a holistic state involving physical, mental, and social well-being, extending beyond the absence of disease. It encompasses an individual's proficiency in various areas: physical, focusing on ease in physical activities; mental, involving clear thinking and concentration; emotional, encompassing moods and reactions; and spiritual, referring to personal beliefs about oneself and the world.

Single parents are at risk for anxiety and depression.

The struggles faced by single parents can be challenging, often leading to feelings of isolation. Single mothers are at a heightened risk of depression and anxiety due to the unique challenges of raising children alone. The absence of a partner's support may contribute to a sense of isolation, stress, and overwhelm, increasing the vulnerability to mental health issues. Factors such as limited social connections, financial stressors, and managing responsibilities alone can contribute to this heightened risk.

Wellness can help fight depression and anxiety.

The positive aspect is that wellness practices can effectively combat depression and anxiety. Engaging in activities such as exercise, meditation, maintaining a balanced diet, and spending time with friends can contribute significantly to improved mental health.

Exercise, in particular, has been shown to reduce stress levels and enhance self-esteem by triggering the release of endorphins, hormones associated with a sense of well-being. Even a short daily exercise of 15 minutes can have a noticeable impact. Studies indicate that regular meditation may rival the effectiveness of antidepressants in addressing mild to moderate depression symptoms. For those struggling with sleep, practicing mindfulness meditation before bedtime can be beneficial.

Additionally, understanding the connection between nutrition and mental health can be explored for further insights. Regular shared meals with family or friends also play a role in stress reduction throughout the day.

Exercise can help reduce stress, improve sleep and boost energy levels by increasing serotonin and dopamine in the brain.

Engaging in regular exercise offers a range of benefits for single parents facing the challenges of balancing work and family life. Exercise has proven effective in reducing stress by lowering cortisol, the body's stress hormone, while simultaneously increasing the release of serotonin and dopamine in the brain. These neurotransmitters contribute to improved mood and happiness. Moreover, exercise has demonstrated its efficacy as a treatment for anxiety disorders, including panic attacks and obsessive-compulsive disorder (OCD).

Notably, exercise plays a crucial role in enhancing sleep quality by regulating the circadian rhythm, the 24-hour cycle governing sleep-wake patterns. A recent study revealed that individuals who exercised regularly experienced longer sleep durations compared to those who did not engage in regular physical activity.

It's worth noting that different types of exercise impact sleep duration uniquely: aerobic workouts contribute to deeper sleep stages, while resistance training enhances REM cycles during sleep. This makes exercise a valuable tool for single parents seeking to manage stress, boost mood, and improve sleep in the midst of their demanding responsibilities.

Mental wellness strategies can also help with talking to kids about difficult topics surrounding divorce, separation and new relationships.

In challenging situations like divorce, separation, and new relationships, incorporating mental wellness strategies can be instrumental in facilitating conversations with children. As a single parent navigating through these changes, addressing such topics with your children may pose difficulties, considering the emotional toll on yourself. Nevertheless, carving out time for these conversations is crucial. Engaging in open and honest dialogue not only fosters trust between you and your child but also provides them with a sense of security amidst the changes they are experiencing. Prioritizing mental wellness strategies in these discussions can contribute to a healthier and more supportive environment for both you and your child.

If you're a single parent, taking care of your mental and physical health is important for everyone in your family.

Prioritizing your mental and physical health is essential for single parents, benefiting not only yourself but your entire family. Engaging in wellness practices aids in managing stress and overcoming various challenges, ultimately supporting you in becoming the parent, employee, or friend you aspire to be. It's noteworthy that wellness doesn't necessarily come with a price tag; simple steps like improving your diet or incorporating more exercise can kickstart this journey. As you witness positive changes in yourself, gradually integrate additional activities, fostering a habit of wellness that contributes to your overall well-being.

If you're a single parent, it can be tough to find time to take care of yourself. You may have many responsibilities that take up your time and energy, or you may have just been so busy taking care of others that now it's time for some self-care. But don't worry! There are ways to make sure that you stay healthy even when life gets crazy. The first step is identifying what kind of wellness means the most to you—whether it's continuing an exercise routine or spending more quality time with friends and family members who support your journey as an individual. Then, put some of the aforementioned strategies into action to transform your goals into realities!

Fitness Tips for Single Parents

Balancing the demands of single parenting with fitness might feel challenging, but prioritizing your well-being is crucial for both your health and your kids' welfare. Consider these ideas to stay fit as a single parent:

Juggling fitness goals can be tough for any parent, and single parents have their own unique set of challenges to navigate.

Balancing a fitness plan can be challenging for anyone, given the demands of daily life. Single parents, particularly single parents, face additional hurdles. Their schedules are tightly packed with managing work, home life, social commitments, and their children's activities. This often leaves very little time for personal workouts. Financial constraints add another layer, as single parents may be navigating child support, alimony, and other bills. Energy levels can also take a hit, given the added stress of sole responsibility for their children's well-being. Despite these challenges, it's crucial not to let them hinder progress towards fitness goals.

1. Remind yourself why you want to get fit.

- Knowing your goals will help you stay motivated and focused on your fitness journey.
- When you know what benefits being fit will bring to your life, it makes it easier to stick with it.
- Why do I want to be fit? What is the benefit of being fit? How will being fit make my life better?

2. Make it a priority, but realistically so.

- Prioritize your fitness goals, but don't let them take over your life. Your kids are more important than getting fit—especially if you're worried about their well-being (and you should be). So don't make excuses for not getting fit; rather, find ways to work around it and set realistic goals for yourself that balance caring for your family with taking care of yourself. Remember: you don't have to do everything at once!

- Don't use your kids as an excuse to not exercise. Kids can be a nuisance when trying to get in a quick workout or run, but if you truly want something done right, then do it yourself—even if it's just going on walks around the neighborhood with them in strollers or pushing them through the park while they ride bikes! The point is that no matter how busy things get around the house or how many times they drive us crazy during our workouts (because let's face it—kids are very good at doing that), we still need time out of those responsibilities so we can feel refreshed and energized again—so what better way than through exercise?

3. Focus on your goals, not successes and failures.

The idea that it's better to focus on the journey rather than the destination can be applied to fitness as well. In fact, it's important to focus on your goals over all else because that will keep you moving forward no matter what setbacks arise along the way. If you've failed at a diet before or if this is just one of many diets you've tried in the past, don't let those experiences discourage you from continuing to work toward your weight loss goal!

Instead, think about how far along you've come since then and use that knowledge to motivate yourself further down the road. Remember: every step is progress toward your goal—no matter how small!

4. If possible, workout at home to save time, money and energy.

One of the challenges of being a single parent is that you don't have as much time to get out and exercise. It can also be tough to find the energy to leave your house when you are already tired from working all day.

You don't need fancy equipment or a gym membership in order to build muscle and burn fat—you just need some basic supplies that you probably already own! Make sure you have:

- A yoga mat
- Dumbbells or resistance bands (to make bodyweight exercises more challenging)
- A kettlebell (for explosive strength training)

5. Don't beat yourself up if you have to miss a workout session or eat something unhealthy one day.

Don't beat yourself up if you have to miss a workout session or eat something unhealthy one day. Just get back on track the next day and don't make excuses for yourself.

Also, don't worry about what others are doing in terms of their exercise habits or diet. It's not like they're watching you and giving you grief when they see that cookie that went down the hatch at 3PM!

6. Keep it simple! The less time and equipment you need, the easier it will be to do the routine every day.

It's important to find an activity that you can do every day, even if it's only for 10 minutes. It doesn't need to be complicated—in fact, the easier it is, the more likely you are to stick with it. Here are some ideas:

- Use a timer on your phone or watch. If you have a smartphone and headphones, this is a great way to go! Just make sure your phone has enough battery power before starting your fitness session. And be sure not to wear earbuds during any other time in public—it's just not safe for others around you (and maybe even illegal).

- Set up a workout buddy who lives near by so that someone else can hold each other accountable for working out at least once per week (or whatever schedule works best). You don't need anything fancy here either—just set up regular meetings where one person leads their own routine while another follows along with theirs nearby. Make sure they know what they're doing though; otherwise there could be injuries!

- Find some free online resources like YouTube videos or blog posts about great fitness routines that anyone can do at home without equipment but still get results fast (like losing weight). These kinds of resources often include pictures showing poses as well as helpful tips throughout each post/video describing how important it is not just physically but mentally too--which means motivating ourselves through visualization techniques instead of just talking ourselves out of going because we think "it won't work." This kind of self-talk needs constant practice especially because most people tend towards negative thoughts instead of focusing on positives which leads them back down paths which aren't healthy either physically OR mentally--so try using positive affirmations whenever possible during these sessions too!

Being a fit single parent is more about consistency than intensity!

Achieving fitness as a single parent is more about consistency than intensity. You don't need to worry; working hard is still very much possible. While it may not be as glamorous as Barry's Bootcamp or SoulCycle, there are effective ways to get active and feel great. Here are some practical examples:

- Incorporate a quick run around the block before dinner each night, or challenge yourself with a run up a hill.
- Opt for stairs instead of an elevator during daily errands; it might even get you to your destination faster!
- When cooking for your family, consider doubling up on food one night per week to ensure everyone gets a second helping without the need to prepare another dish from scratch. This way, leftovers for lunch are sorted for everyone!

Consistency is key for a fit single parent. Stick to your fitness plan and prioritize healthy eating as often as you can. Don't stress about others' opinions. Remember, it's more about staying consistent than pushing yourself too hard. On days when a full workout feels challenging, opt for something active like a refreshing walk. The beauty of this routine? You'll experience both physical and mental well-being by staying committed!

CHAPTER 3

Dollars and Sense: Smart Money Management for Single Parents

Budgeting and Money Management Tips for Single Parents

Navigating budgeting and money management as a single parent may seem daunting, but fear not! There are numerous strategies to save on child care, transportation, groceries, and essentials without compromising your quality of life. I've gathered a list of my top tips to help you make ends meet as a single parent:

Save money on child care by taking advantage of every program you can.

Regardless of your income, a significant portion of your earnings likely goes towards child care expenses. In the United States, the average annual cost of daycare is around $14,000+, not accounting for additional expenses like transportation or school-related costs. However, there's hope! Numerous resources are available for single parents seeking affordable child care options. Here are some tips to help you save money on child care, allowing you to allocate more funds to other essential needs:

1. Leverage available programs: Child care assistance initiatives such as Head Start and Early Head Start offer free or low-cost preschool options for children under three years old. These programs also aid in finding quality child care providers who accept government vouchers or

offer tax credits through the Child and Dependent Care Tax Credit Program (CDCTC).

2. Tax credits: If your family's income exceeds the eligibility criteria for certain programs, explore tax credits like Dependent Care Expenses (DCE) and Earned Income Tax Credit (EITC). These credits can provide up to 40 percent off annual daycare expenses when filed correctly within specified deadlines mandated by law.

Carpool when possible to save on gas and reduce wear and tear on your car.

Living in a city? Carpooling is a money-saving strategy for cutting down on gas and parking expenses. For those in rural areas, carpooling is still beneficial as it minimizes wear and tear on your vehicle. If your kids are old enough to drive, involving them in the driving responsibilities can further alleviate costs.

Take advantage of free entertainment, like libraries and community events.

- Take advantage of free entertainment, like libraries and community events.
- Take advantage of free activities like reading, cooking and gardening.
- Look into free resources online (like singlemomssociety.com).

Use coupons and buy in bulk whenever possible to save money on groceries.

Utilizing coupons is an effective way to cut costs on groceries. Opt for bulk purchases when feasible, saving both time and money. Take advantage of sales to stock up on items for an extended period. Opt for store brand products over name brands for a cost-effective alternative with comparable quality. When feasible, prioritize seasonal food items to benefit from lower prices due to limited availability during specific times of the year.

Teach your kids about budgeting.

Instilling budgeting skills in your family is crucial for understanding the value of money and making prudent financial decisions. Introduce the concept of saving, emphasizing that setting aside a portion of their earnings or gifts enables them to have more flexibility for future expenses. Demonstrate the potential interest growth by placing their savings in a bank account, mutual fund, or stock portfolio, providing them with greater financial freedom over time.

Visit food banks, food pantries and thrift stores for clothing, toys and household items.

You can acquire essential items for your children and household without breaking the bank by exploring food banks, food pantries, and thrift stores. Whether you need toys, clothes, basic household essentials, or furniture, these options offer budget-friendly solutions to help you save money.

Pay down credit card debt as quickly as possible to reduce interest payments.

Using credit cards can be beneficial for building financial stability, but it can become a debt trap if spending isn't monitored. Despite paying off the balance each month, the interest rates can accumulate substantial additional costs over time. Additionally, managing multiple credit cards with various balances can lead to swift accrual of small charges, contributing to financial challenges

Keep your job skills up-to-date so that you have multiple sources of income if you need them.

Maintaining updated skills is crucial, especially during periods of unemployment. Instead of waiting, be proactive in exploring opportunities to enhance your employability.

Embrace learning new things or taking diverse classes, even if they differ from your current expertise. Keep an open mind for opportunities that not only bring in additional income but also augment your value as an employee or business owner.

Thinking beyond conventional methods and considering various options will contribute to financial stability and broaden your avenues for income generation.

Brown bag it as much as possible instead of eating out at restaurants.

Opt for brown bagging your meals instead of dining out at restaurants. Not only does it save money, but it also promotes healthier eating habits. Embracing the practice of brown bagging serves as an excellent opportunity to instill frugality in your kids and is an effective means to cut down on food expenses.

Find ways to make extra money through side jobs, such as waiting tables or tutoring. If you have a hobby that can make money, this is a way to earn some cash while doing something you love.

Explore opportunities to earn extra income through side jobs, such as transcribing or tutoring. If you possess a hobby that can be monetized, turning it into a source of income allows you to combine passion with financial gain. Additionally, consider the possibility of starting your own business. Many single parents have successfully built thriving businesses from the ground up, initially with modest resources. Don't hesitate to seek support from friends, family, neighbors, or even acquaintances who may have experience in small business ownership – people often find joy in assisting others in need.

See if your employer will pay for courses that improve your job skills or allow you extra time to study for college classes that will help advance your career goals. This is an excellent way to find the means to pay for post-secondary education without having to take out student loans for tuition, books and fees.

Check if your employer offers support for courses that enhance your job skills or provides additional time for studying college classes that align with your career objectives. This can be a valuable avenue for financing higher education without resorting to student loans to cover tuition, books, and fees. With luck, your employer may have tuition reimbursement programs, flexible work schedules accommodating school attendance, and options for remote work or job sharing with colleagues pursuing part-time college studies while maintaining full-time employment.

Additional Budgeting Tips:

1. Craft a Practical Budget:

- Develop a comprehensive budget that encompasses all your monthly expenses, from housing and utilities to childcare and groceries. Ensure your budget aligns realistically with your income, prioritizing essential needs.

2. Build an Emergency Fund:

- Establish an emergency fund to cushion unforeseen expenses. Strive to save three to six months' worth of living expenses. This financial buffer can prove invaluable during unexpected challenges.

3. Explore Child Support Options:

- If applicable, explore legal avenues to secure child support from the noncustodial parent. Understanding your rights and seeking professional advice ensures the financial needs of your child are met.

4. Tap into Government Assistance:

- Investigate government assistance programs offering financial support for single parents. This may include assistance with food, housing, and healthcare costs.

5. Conquer Debt Strategically:

- Develop a strategic plan for repaying outstanding debts. Prioritize high-interest debts while maintaining minimum payments on others. This approach can save you money over time.

6. Save for Future Milestones:

- Plan for the future by saving for your child's education or your own retirement. Designate specific savings accounts for these goals to track progress effectively.

7. Regular Budget Reviews:

- Regularly review and adjust your budget to reflect changes in your life circumstances. A flexible budget ensures you can adapt to the evolving needs of your family.

8. Embrace Flexible Work Options:

- Consider flexible work arrangements, such as remote work or adjusted hours, to strike a balance between career responsibilities and parenting duties.

9. Secure Comprehensive Insurance:

- Ensure you have sufficient insurance coverage for health, property, and life. This provides crucial protection against unforeseen circumstances for you and your children.

10. Empower Through Financial Literacy:

- Instill financial literacy in your children early on. Teaching them about budgeting, saving, and responsible spending empowers them to make informed financial decisions in the future.

11. Leverage Support Services:

- Take advantage of community resources and support services. Local nonprofits and community organizations may offer financial assistance, counseling, or workshops tailored to support single parents.

By implementing these tips, you can navigate the financial landscape with finesse, fostering stability for both you and your children. Remember, seeking professional advice and adapting these tips to your specific situation can lead to greater financial well-being.

There you have it – practical tips and tricks for single parents to budget more effectively. Budgeting may not always be easy, but by implementing these strategies, single parents can save money on essentials like child care, groceries, and entertainment. If you need additional assistance with managing your finances, consider reaching out to your accountant or financial planner for personalized advice. Don't forget to start building an emergency fund to handle unexpected expenses related to your car or home.

CHAPTER 4

Learning and Earning: A Single Parent's Guide to Education and Career

Education and Single Parents

Let's discuss education for single parents and how to pursue your dreams while ensuring your children's needs are met.

Figure Out What You Need

Once you've explored the available programs, it's essential to tailor your choice to your family's needs. Consider the program's focus, whether it leans more towards education or career advancement, aligning it with your goals. Factor in costs, as some programs may have fees, while others don't. Ensure you meet any application requirements, and if time commitments differ between online and face-to-face classes, weigh the pros and cons based on your circumstances. It's crucial to make informed decisions that align with both your aspirations and your family's well-being

Set Realistic Goals

- Set a goal to complete a degree or certificate.
- Make sure you're realistic in terms of your timeline and resources, especially since you may need to work full-time while going to school.

- Don't go more than one year over the time it takes for your program to be completed, unless you're willing to pay for it out of pocket.
- If you want some direction on what kind of school might be best for single parents,, look up factors such as accreditation (is it regionally accredited?), student population (do they have any programs specifically designed for single parents?), and campus location (where's the closest city?).

Get Organized

Create a priority list, outlining essential tasks categorized by urgency, such as daily or weekly responsibilities. Plan the sequence of these tasks to ensure timely completion. For instance, if you have a doctor's appointment on Monday at 11 am, prioritize it at the top of your list for that day. Utilize a planner or calendar to document appointments, deadlines, and recurring tasks. This tool can help you stay organized, ensuring nothing vital is overlooked, from routine chores to significant events like birthdays or doctor's appointments. Keep your plans visible and accessible for effective time management.

Line Up Child Care

Facing the fear of finding and affording quality child care is a common concern, but numerous resources can assist you in this journey. Conduct thorough research, examining provider rates and seeking recommendations from friends, family, or local community centers.

Explore online platforms like Child Care Aware® of America, offering free information on high-quality child care and financial assistance options such as subsidies, tax credits, and deductions.

Parents Anonymous® provides support groups for mothers facing similar challenges.

Additionally, check the Child Care Subsidy Locator Service to determine eligibility for assistance programs like Temporary Assistance to Needy Families (TANF). Connecting with your state's TANF agency at 1-877-638-8532 can provide insights into available childcare support.

Explore Financial Aid

Exploring financial aid options is crucial for supporting your education, and various avenues exist for assistance. Start by completing the FAFSA form to determine eligibility for federal or state funding. If public assistance is not available, explore private scholarships as a potential alternative. Additionally, look into grants offered by your university or employer-sponsored programs before considering private loans, which may have less favorable terms. If none of these options appear suitable initially, taking a temporary break from school could help reduce your student debt load when it's time to commence repayment.

Apply for Scholarships

Scholarships serve as financial assistance provided by schools or organizations, often considering factors like academic achievement, demographics, or financial need. To apply for scholarships, visit the organization's website, and if not available, find their contact information via a directory search. Call and inquire about scholarships for individuals in your demographic, or ask for referrals to other potential sources. If not awarded a scholarship, there are alternative funding options like loans, grants from schools, federal aid through FAFSA, and work-study programs.

Attend Classes Online

Online classes provide a convenient and flexible option for single parents managing child care responsibilities and work schedules. With the ability to take classes at any time, from any location, online education offers a feasible path to pursue a degree or certificate while balancing family commitments. Western Governors University is a reputable online institution that offers flexible education options, catering to the needs of single parents. Explore such institutions to find programs that align with your schedule and educational goals.

Ask for Help

When navigating the challenges of single parenthood, seeking help is crucial. Reach out to family and friends who may offer support, whether through babysitting or financial assistance. Additionally, engage with teachers or school staff for extra support in the classroom or access to community resources. Discussing potential aid options with your school counselor, both on campus and in the broader community, can provide valuable assistance, such as scholarships or programs like Head Start.

With a little planning, there are programs to help you pursue your education.

Explore various public and private programs that offer financial aid for education, including scholarships. Many universities provide support, especially for single mothers returning to school. Online classes offer advantages such as saving time, money, and reducing stress associated with commuting and crowded classrooms.

Balancing parenthood and education can be challenging, but with realistic goals and effective time management, it's possible for single parents to pursue education and successfully build a better future for themselves and their families.

CHAPTER 5

Business/Entrepreneurship for Single Parents

Business Development for Single Parents

Starting your own business as a single mom can offer flexibility and help with childcare expenses. Consider these tips to get started on your entrepreneurial journey.

Do Your Homework

Consider the competition in your field and find ways to make your business stand out. Reflect on why you want to start your own business and explore ways to set yourself apart. Understand your audience, focus on their needs, and make sure your offerings resonate with them. Stay updated on market trends to align your business with success, and check statistics on similar companies for informed decision-making

Don't Be Afraid To Ask for Help

Be open to accepting help from those willing to offer it, even if it's not exactly what you envisioned. Family and friends may not have specific expertise but can provide valuable moral support. Check with local government agencies for resources available to start-up businesses, including workshops. Connect with local business associations for networking opportunities and shared insights on running successful companies

Choose the right business

Choose a business that aligns with your passions and skills, considering whether others have tried similar ideas. Be cautious of businesses with high startup costs, as they may not be sustainable. Evaluate the time commitment required and ensure it fits with your schedule before making financial or emotional commitments.

Take advantage of resources available to you

Embrace the learning curve of starting a business by tapping into free or affordable resources like business incubators and co-working spaces. Explore grants and government programs that offer seed capital for small businesses with growth potential, such as SBIR and STTR. Remember, the key is taking action and not letting fear of failure hold you back from pursuing your dream of owning a business.

Start it yourself!

Take the initiative to start your own business by either launching a side hustle or turning a skill you already possess into a full-fledged venture. Equip yourself with new skills through online courses, particularly focusing on website development and effective marketing. Establish a distinctive brand presence using social media marketing, whether it's through becoming an influencer on platforms like Instagram or YouTube or utilizing Facebook ads to reach your target audience effectively.

Owning your own business can be a great thing for single parents.

Running your own business as a single parent offers the flexibility to work around your kids' schedules, set your own hours, and make independent decisions. While it may pose initial challenges compared to a dual-income scenario, there are numerous avenues for single parents to thrive and become successful entrepreneurs.

How To Access Business Resources:

- Search for online resources dedicated to single parents in business.
- Explore websites, forums, and platforms that offer advice, support, and resources for single-parent entrepreneurs.

1. Government Programs:

- Check government websites for programs supporting single parents in business.
- Investigate Small Business Administration (SBA) resources and grants that might be available specifically for single parents.

2. Local Support Organizations:

- Connect with local chambers of commerce, women's business networks, or single-parent support groups.
- Attend local events or workshops that focus on entrepreneurship and business development for single parents.

3. Business Incubators for Parents:

- Look for business incubators or accelerators that cater to parents, providing support, mentorship, and resources specific to their needs.

4. Parenting and Business Blogs:

- Follow blogs or websites that share stories and advice from single parents who have successfully navigated entrepreneurship.

- Look for tips on balancing parenting responsibilities with running a business.

5. Networking Groups:
- Join online and local networking groups for single parents in business.
- Engage with other entrepreneurs, share experiences, and seek advice from those who have faced similar challenges.

6. Financial Assistance Programs:
- Explore financial assistance programs or grants designed to support single parents entering or growing their businesses.

7. Educational Resources:
- Seek out educational resources tailored for single parents, such as online courses or workshops addressing business development topics.

8. Mentorship Programs:
- Explore mentorship programs that connect single-parent entrepreneurs with experienced mentors who can provide guidance and support.

9. Local Community Resources:
- Check with local community centers, libraries, or women's organizations for resources and workshops aimed at supporting single parents in business

Embarking on business ownership may make you nervous, but don't let that hesitation hinder you. It's a fantastic opportunity for single parents to forge their own path and take control of their lives. Remember, the first step is often the most challenging, but once you overcome that initial fear, things tend to fall into place more smoothly than expected!

Self-Employed Parents

Explore the wealth of resources available for self-employed parents to boost your business journey. Connect with fellow parents in online forums or forge local community ties with other business owners. These connections can be instrumental in creating a supportive network for your business success.

Mompreneurs Worldwide:

Mompreneurs Worldwide is a great resource for moms who are interested in starting a business. The website has lots of articles, videos and podcasts to help you get started. They also have a forum where moms can ask questions and get answers. You can use the site's directory of other resources if you need help with anything else while running your business.

Women Entrepreneurs:

Connect with women entrepreneurs to tap into their wealth of experience in starting and running businesses, particularly women-owned businesses. Gain valuable insights by asking about their entrepreneurial journey, strategies for business management, and how they've overcome challenges. Learning from their extensive experience can provide valuable lessons, especially if you're navigating unfamiliar aspects of entrepreneurship, such as marketing strategies. Building connections with women entrepreneurs creates an opportunity for mentorship and shared wisdom in your own business endeavors.

LinkedIn and Networking Groups: Joining professional networks on platforms like LinkedIn can connect you with fellow entrepreneurs and industry professionals. Look for groups or forums where you can share experiences and gain insights.

SCORE: SCORE is a nonprofit organization that provides mentoring to small business owners. You can connect with a mentor who can offer guidance on various aspects of entrepreneurship.

Small Business Administration (SBA): The SBA offers a wealth of resources for entrepreneurs, including guides, webinars, and local assistance. Explore their website for information tailored to your business needs.

Dadpreneur Community: While not a specific platform, consider searching for communities or forums where dad entrepreneurs share their experiences. Websites like Reddit might have relevant subreddits or forums.

Online Courses and Webinars: Platforms like Coursera, Udemy, and Skillshare offer courses on various aspects of business, from marketing to finance. These can help you enhance your skills and knowledge.

Dadpreneur Hub: A dynamic community of entrepreneurs and business leaders who are committed to supporting one another in achieving their business goals. The mission is to provide members with the resources, connections, and support they need to succeed. The belief is that by working together, they can achieve more than they ever could alone.

Dad-specific Blogs and Websites: Look for blogs or websites that focus on the experiences of dad entrepreneurs. These platforms may share insights, tips, and success stories from fellow single dads in business.

Business Boutique: If you're a mom looking to kickstart your business journey, Business Boutique is an excellent resource. Access free templates for business plans, marketing strategies, and social media plans to help bring your ideas to life. Additionally, explore their ebook offering valuable tips on starting your own business, tailored for single moms. Business Boutique provides practical tools and insights to support you on your entrepreneurial path.

Mommy Millionaire: Explore Mommy Millionaire, a blog dedicated to empowering moms to earn money from home. Founded by Nancy Laidlaw, featured on CNN and ABC News, it offers valuable benefits, including access to a supportive community of moms venturing into entrepreneurship. Members enjoy perks like a free guide on launching an online business from scratch, complete with templates and step-by-step instructions. Mommy Millionaire also provides exclusive discounts on essential business tools, making entrepreneurship more accessible

There are tons of resources for single parents to start a business. You can find them online, through your local Chamber of Commerce and inquiring with other mompreneurs and dadpreneurs in your community If you're looking for mentorship, there are also great resources out there to help you find it.

Conclusion

In essence, this chapter serves as a compass for single mompreneurs and dadpreneurs, offering insights, practical tips, and a supportive voice. As they navigate the exciting yet demanding terrain of building businesses while raising children, may they find encouragement, inspiration, and a community that understands the unique challenges and triumphs they face.

CHAPTER 6

Navigating Unleashing Potential: Single Parenthood and Disability

Parenthood is a journey filled with joys, challenges, and unexpected twists, and for single parents navigating it with disabilities, the journey may seem even more daunting. In this chapter, we'll delve into the unique experiences and practical strategies for single parents with disabilities, including those who are parenting children with disabilities themselves. We'll address the complexities of managing both roles solo, offering specific resources and referrals to help navigate the journey more effectively.

Embracing Parenthood with Disabilities

Every family is unique, and being a single parent with a disability adds a layer of diversity to the parenting experience. Embrace your strengths and acknowledge the resilience it takes to raise children solo while managing a disability.

Embracing the diversity within families is a beautiful aspect of parenting.

As a single parent with a disability, your journey is uniquely yours, adding depth and richness to the tapestry of parenthood. Recognize the strengths you bring to the table and honor the resilience it takes to navigate the challenges of raising children solo while managing a disability. You are a testament to the beauty of diversity and the limitless capacity of the human spirit to overcome obstacles with grace and determination.

Celebrating the diversity within families is a wonderful part of the parenting experience. As a single parent with a disability, your journey brings a unique perspective and strength to the table. Embrace the strengths you possess and acknowledge the resilience it takes to navigate parenthood solo while managing a disability. Your journey is a testament to the beauty of diversity and the incredible power within you to overcome challenges with courage and grace.

Finding Inner Strength

Finding your inner strength is crucial as you navigate the challenges of single parenting with a disability. Despite the obstacles you may face, know that you hold a reservoir of resilience within you that empowers you to overcome any hurdle and flourish as a parent. Draw inspiration from the stories of other single parents with disabilities who have triumphed over similar challenges, and let their journeys inspire and motivate you on your path. Together, we can find strength in solidarity and conquer whatever obstacles may come our way.

Discovering your inner strength is pivotal as you journey through the complexities of single parenting with a disability. Despite the hurdles you encounter, remember that deep within you lies a wellspring of resilience, guiding you to surmount challenges and thrive as a parent. Take solace in the stories of fellow single parents with disabilities who have bravely navigated similar paths, drawing inspiration from their triumphs and finding solidarity in shared experiences. Together, let us harness the power of our collective strength to navigate this journey with courage and resilience.

Despite the challenges, remember that you possess an inner strength that enables you to overcome obstacles and thrive as a parent.

Parenting is an incredible journey, but when you're a single parent with a disability, it can feel like climbing a mountain with extra weight on your shoulders. However, there are ways to make this journey not only manageable but fulfilling. Here are some friendly tips:

- Nourish Yourself: You can't pour from an empty cup. Remember to take care of yourself first. Whether it's a bubble bath, a walk in nature, or a chat with a friend, find what replenishes your spirit and prioritize it.

- Parenting on Your Terms: There's no one-size-fits-all approach to parenting, especially when you're juggling a disability. Embrace the flexibility to parent in a way that works best for you and your child. That might mean using adaptive tools, creating unique routines, or finding your own creative solutions.

- Lean on Your Tribe: You don't have to do this alone. Build a strong support system of friends, family, and professionals who understand your challenges and are there to lend a hand when needed. And don't forget the power of online communities—they can be a lifeline for support and encouragement.

- Be Your Own Advocate: Accessibility matters. Don't hesitate to speak up for the accommodations you need to parent effectively. Whether it's advocating for inclusive policies or ensuring accessible facilities, your voice is a powerful tool for change.

- Honest Conversations: Your child is part of this journey too. Be open and honest with them about your disability. Answer their questions, address their concerns, and reassure them that your love and ability to care for them are unwavering.
- Ask for Help: Superheroes need backup too. Don't be afraid to reach out for professional assistance when necessary. Whether it's hiring caregivers or utilizing respite care services, getting the support you need is a sign of strength, not weakness.
- Set Realistic Expectations: Rome wasn't built in a day, and neither is perfect parenting. Be kind to yourself and set realistic expectations. Focus on what you can accomplish, celebrate your victories, and let go of the guilt when things don't go as planned.
- Celebrate Every Win: Big or small, every victory deserves a celebration. Parenting with a disability is no easy feat, and you deserve to pat yourself on the back for all the hard work and love you pour into your child every single day.

Remember, you're not just surviving—you're thriving. And by embracing your uniqueness, advocating for your needs, and surrounding yourself with support, you're showing your child what true resilience looks like. Keep shining,

Parenting Children with Disabilities as a Single Parent

Understanding Your Child's Needs:

Parenting a child with disabilities is a journey filled with unique challenges and opportunities for growth. One of the most crucial aspects of this journey is understanding your child's needs. This involves not only recognizing their physical and emotional requirements but also navigating the complex landscape of medical appointments, therapies, and educational support.

As a parent, educating yourself about your child's specific condition is paramount. Take the time to research and learn about the medical aspects of their disability, as well as the potential challenges they may face in daily life. Understanding the intricacies of their condition will not only help you provide better care but also empower you to advocate effectively on their behalf.

In addition to educating yourself, connecting with other parents or support groups can provide invaluable guidance and encouragement. Sharing experiences and insights with those who have walked a similar path can offer reassurance, practical advice, and a sense of community. Whether it's attending support group meetings, participating in online forums, or joining local parent networks, surrounding yourself with a supportive community can make a world of difference in navigating the complexities of parenting a child with disabilities.

Here are some specific tips and expert advice for understanding and meeting your child's needs as a parent of a child with disabilities:

- Educate Yourself: Take the time to research and learn about your child's specific disability. Understand the medical aspects, potential challenges, and available resources. Knowledge is power, and being informed will empower you to make informed decisions and advocate effectively for your child.

- Seek Professional Guidance: Consult with healthcare professionals, therapists, and educators who specialize in your child's condition. They can offer valuable insights, guidance, and support tailored to your child's unique needs. Don't hesitate to ask questions and seek clarification on any aspect of your child's care or treatment plan.

- Create a Support Network: Surround yourself with a supportive network of family, friends, and professionals who understand your child's needs and can offer assistance when needed. Joining support groups or online communities for parents of children with disabilities can provide invaluable emotional support, practical advice, and a sense of camaraderie.

- Establish Open Communication: Foster open and honest communication with your child about their disability. Encourage them to ask questions, express their feelings, and voice any concerns they may have. Create a safe and supportive environment where they feel comfortable discussing their needs and seeking assistance when necessary.

- Advocate for Your Child: Be your child's strongest advocate, ensuring that their needs are met and their rights are protected. Advocate for inclusive education, accessible facilities, and accommodations that support your child's learning and development. Don't be afraid to speak up and assertively communicate your child's needs to teachers, healthcare providers, and other stakeholders.

- Promote Independence: Encourage your child to develop independence and self-advocacy skills from an early age. Provide opportunities for them to make choices, solve problems, and take on age-appropriate responsibilities. Foster a sense of confidence and self-esteem as they navigate the challenges of living with a disability.

- Celebrate Progress: Celebrate your child's achievements, no matter how small. Recognize their strengths, resilience, and progress as they overcome obstacles and reach milestones. Celebrating their successes will boost their confidence and motivation, reinforcing their belief in their own abilities.

- Take Care of Yourself: Lastly, remember to prioritize self-care. Parenting a child with disabilities can be physically, emotionally, and mentally demanding. Take breaks when needed, seek support from others, and engage in activities that rejuvenate and replenish your spirit. By taking care of yourself, you'll be better equipped to care for your child and meet their needs effectively.

By following these tips and seeking support from professionals and your support network, you can better understand and meet your child's needs as a parent of a child with disabilities. Remember, you are not alone on this journey, and together, we can create a supportive and nurturing environment where all children can thrive.

Advocating for Inclusion and Accessibility

As a single parent with a disability, advocating for accessibility and inclusion is not just about making life easier for yourself—it's about creating a more equitable world for all. By championing accessibility, educating others, and empowering your child, you can make a lasting impact on your community and beyond.

Advocating for inclusive policies and accessible facilities is essential for ensuring that both you and your child can fully participate in community life. Whether it's advocating for wheelchair ramps, accessible parking spaces, or braille signage, every step towards greater accessibility benefits not only individuals with disabilities but society as a whole. Get involved in disability rights organizations or parent advocacy groups to lobby for changes that benefit single parents and children with disabilities. Together, we can work towards a more inclusive and accessible future for everyone.

Educating Others:

Taking the opportunity to educate others about disability issues is a powerful way to promote understanding and acceptance. Share your experiences openly and honestly, and encourage conversations about inclusion and accessibility. By raising awareness about the unique needs and challenges faced by single parents and children with disabilities, you can help break down stereotypes and foster a more inclusive community where everyone feels valued and respected.

Empowering Your Child:

Empowering your child is perhaps the most important gift you can give them. Instill confidence and resilience by advocating for their needs and celebrating their strengths. Encourage them to embrace their uniqueness and to advocate for themselves as they navigate the world. Teach them that their disability does not define them, but rather adds to the richness of who they are. By empowering your child to be their own advocate, you are equipping them with the skills and confidence they need to thrive in any situation.

Navigating single parenthood with disabilities, especially when parenting a child with disabilities, presents unique challenges. However, with the right support and resources, it's possible to thrive and create a loving, nurturing environment for yourself and your children. By embracing your unique abilities, advocating for inclusion and accessibility, and prioritizing self-care, you can overcome obstacles and enjoy the journey of parenthood to the fullest. Remember, you're not alone, and there are plenty of specific resources and referrals available to support you on this incredible journey.

Resources:

- Disability Organizations:
- National Organization on Disability (NOD) - www.nod.org
- Disabled Parenting Project - www.disabledparenting.com
- Parenting Support Groups:
- Single Parent Advocate - www.singleparentadvocate.org
- Parents with Disabilities Online - www.parentswithdisabilities.com
- Social Services Agencies:
- Department of Social Services (DSS)
- Centers for Independent Living (CILs)
- Respite Care Services:
- National Respite Locator Service - www.archrespite.org/respitelocator

Booklist:

- Parenting With Disabilities: A Positive Approach" by Colleen M. Arnold
- "The Special Needs Parent Handbook: Critical Strategies and Practical Advice to Help You Survive and Thrive" by Jonathan Singer
- "The Single Parent's Handbook: Lessons in Love, Life, and Livelihood" by Katherine Baldwin
- "Parenting Through the Storm: How to Handle the Highs, the Lows, and Everything in Between" by Ann Douglas
- "Disabled Parenting: A Guide for an Empowered Life" by Laurie Frank
- "Parenting Beyond Belief: On Raising Ethical, Caring Kids Without Religion" by Dale McGowan (addresses parenting challenges, including those faced by parents with disabilities)
- "Parenting Children with Disabilities: A Professional Source for Hope, Support, and Practical Advice" by Lianne Holliday Willey
- "The Special Needs Parenting Survival Guide: How to Cope with Stress, Keep Up with Your Child's Special Needs, and Thrive" by Susan Senator
- "Parenting Your Complex Child: Become a Powerful Advocate for the Autistic, Down Syndrome, PDD, Bipolar, or Other Special-Needs Child" by Peggy Lou Morgan
- "The Single Mom's Guide to Raising Remarkable Boys" by Gina Panettieri (for single mothers with disabled children, offering insights and practical advice)

CHAPTER 7

Empowering Resilience: Navigating Single Parenthood Through Domestic Challenges

Entering the realm of single parenthood brings a mix of excitement and uncertainty, like stepping onto a new stage with a script yet to be written. However, when faced with the harsh reality of domestic abuse, the script takes an unexpected turn, weaving a narrative fraught with challenges and obstacles. In this chapter, we're delving into the dynamic landscape of single parenthood while navigating the complexities of domestic abuse. We'll uncover the warning signs, map out pathways to safety, and unveil the network of support and resources available. From deciphering the intricacies of abuse to fostering a journey of healing and empowerment, let's embark on this chapter together, forging a path toward a future of safety, strength, and newfound resilience.

Recognizing Domestic Abuse

Understanding the different forms of abuse is crucial for identifying and addressing domestic abuse effectively. Abuse can take on many forms, each with its own set of signs and consequences. It's important to educate yourself about these different types of abuse and to recognize the signs, no matter how subtle they may seem.

- Physical Abuse: This type of abuse involves any form of physical harm or violence inflicted upon a person. It can include hitting, punching, kicking, slapping, or any other act that causes bodily harm or injury. Signs of physical abuse may include unexplained bruises, cuts, or injuries, as well as a pattern of injuries that cannot be easily explained.

- Emotional Abuse: Emotional abuse is characterized by behavior that undermines a person's self-worth, confidence, and emotional well-being. It can involve verbal attacks, insults, manipulation, gaslighting, and constant criticism. Signs of emotional abuse may include low self-esteem, anxiety, depression, and feelings of worthlessness or hopelessness.

- Verbal Abuse: Verbal abuse involves the use of words to intimidate, control, or belittle a person. It can include yelling, screaming, name-calling, threats, and insults. Verbal abuse can have a profound impact on a person's mental and emotional health, leading to feelings of fear, shame, and insecurity.

- Sexual Abuse: Sexual abuse involves any unwanted sexual activity or coercion inflicted upon a person without their consent. It can include rape, sexual assault, molestation, and other forms of sexual violence. Signs of sexual abuse may include physical injuries, changes in behavior, and avoidance of certain situations or people.

- Financial Abuse: Financial abuse occurs when one person controls or exploits another person's finances for their own gain. It can involve withholding money, limiting access to resources, stealing or misusing funds, and preventing the victim from working or earning an income. Financial abuse can leave the victim feeling dependent, trapped, and unable to escape the abusive relationship.

Trusting Your Instincts

Trusting your instincts is key in recognizing early warning signs of abuse. If something feels off in your relationship, listen to that inner voice and pay attention to red flags such as controlling behavior, manipulation, threats, or isolation tactics. Your safety and well-being should always be your top priority.

Seeking help is a crucial step in breaking free from the cycle of abuse. Don't suffer in silence – reach out to trusted friends, family members, or domestic violence hotlines for support and guidance. Remember, you are not alone, and help is available to assist you in navigating this difficult time.

Prioritizing safety is paramount in protecting yourself and your children from harm. Develop a safety plan to prepare for emergencies, including identifying safe spaces, establishing a code word with trusted individuals, and keeping important documents and emergency supplies easily accessible.

Setting boundaries with the abuser is essential for protecting yourself and enforcing consequences for any violations. Your safety and well-being should always come first, and it's important to communicate your boundaries clearly and firmly.

Utilizing legal resources can provide additional support and protection. Familiarize yourself with legal options for obtaining protection orders or restraining orders against the abuser, and seek guidance from legal aid services or domestic violence advocacy organizations. Remember, you have rights, and there are resources available to help you take the necessary steps to ensure your safety and well-being.

Seeking Support and Healing

Seeking support and healing is essential for moving forward and rebuilding your life after experiencing domestic abuse. Connecting with support services can provide invaluable assistance during this challenging time. Reach out to local domestic violence shelters, support groups, and counseling services for survivors of abuse. These organizations offer emotional support, safety planning assistance, and resources to help you navigate the healing process and rebuild your life.

Prioritizing self-care is crucial for your overall well-being and recovery. Invest in activities that nurture your mind, body, and spirit, such as meditation, journaling, exercise, or therapy. Healing from the trauma of domestic abuse takes time, but with patience and self-compassion, you can reclaim your sense of self and find inner peace.

Empowering your children is also important in helping them heal from the effects of abuse. Help them understand the dynamics of abuse and empower them to speak up if they ever feel unsafe. Encourage open communication, provide age-appropriate support, and seek therapy or counseling for them as needed. By providing a supportive and nurturing environment, you can help your children heal and thrive as they navigate their own journey of recovery.

Resources:

- National Domestic Violence Hotline: 1-800-799-SAFE (7233)
- National Coalition Against Domestic Violence: www.ncadv.org

- DomesticShelters.org: www.domesticshelters.org
- Legal Aid Services: Contact your local legal aid organization for assistance with legal matters related to domestic abuse.
- Counseling and Therapy Services: Seek counseling or therapy services for yourself and your children to process the trauma of domestic abuse and work towards healing.

Booklist:

- Why Does He Do That?: Inside the Minds of Angry and Controlling Men" by Lundy Bancroft - This book offers invaluable insights into the mindset of abusive partners and provides strategies for recognizing and responding to abusive behavior.
- "The Verbally Abusive Relationship: How to Recognize It and How to Respond" by Patricia Evans - Focusing on verbal abuse, this book helps readers identify patterns of verbal abuse and offers practical guidance for setting boundaries and protecting oneself.
- "When Dad Hurts Mom: Helping Your Children Heal the Wounds of Witnessing Abuse" by Lundy Bancroft - Written specifically for parents, this book addresses the impact of domestic violence on children and provides strategies for helping them heal from the trauma.
- "It's My Life Now: Starting Over After an Abusive Relationship or Domestic Violence" by Meg Kennedy Dugan and Roger R. Hock - This book offers practical advice and support for survivors of domestic violence as they navigate the process of rebuilding their lives.

- "Breaking Free: Help for Survivors of Child Sexual Abuse" by Carolyn Ainscough and Kay Toon - While focused on child sexual abuse, this book offers valuable insights and support for survivors of abuse seeking healing and recovery.
- "The Courage to Heal: A Guide for Women Survivors of Child Sexual Abuse" by Ellen Bass and Laura Davis - Another resource focused on survivors of sexual abuse, this book provides guidance and support for women on their journey toward healing and reclaiming their lives.

CHAPTER 8

Navigating New Beginnings: Divorce, Dating, and Building a Support Network

Facing news that your marriage is in turmoil can be overwhelmingly disheartening. It might seem like finding a starting point is like searching for a needle in a haystack. However, I want to reassure you that divorce, though undoubtedly a challenging journey, doesn't have to be as insurmountable as it might initially appear. I've personally experienced this. With the right information about the divorce process and guidance from someone with experience, you can navigate this difficult situation with a sense of calm and assurance, making decisions that prioritize the well-being of your family.

Preparing for Divorce

If you find yourself going through a divorce, start by creating a thorough list of what you own and owe. This helps ensure a fair split of assets like furniture or the family car. Also, consider the financial side, like legal fees. Decide if you need a lawyer or mediator to assist during this process.

No matter the situation, follow these steps:

1. Keep all financial records like bank statements and receipts for shared items during the marriage.

2. Understand each party's income to agree on a fair financial arrangement.

Dividing the Assets

Divorce is a complex process that varies for each individual, involving emotional, financial, and time considerations. Different scenarios may arise, such as being single and seeking marriage, having children in a marriage, dealing with a partner's death, or one spouse moving out of state.

Key divorce scenarios include:

1. Single, looking to get married.
2. Married with children.
3. Partner's death.
4. Separation leading to divorce.
5. Divorced with children.
6. Seeking a new marriage after many years.

The first step involves clarifying your divorce goals, considering waiting periods, deciding on legal assistance, and planning for financial implications.

Who Gets What?

If you have no significant assets, navigating the divorce process becomes relatively straightforward. In cases where both spouses have been employed without having children together, each is entitled to half of the earnings accumulated during the marriage. This formula applies if:

- You did not share children with your ex-spouse, or

In cases without children involved, but born before 2008, where one parent received primary physical custody, that parent gets an additional one-third share.

In divorces with children, the court considers child support and custody orders to determine the distribution of assets. If you have an agreement that needs court approval, visit our divorce laws page for guidance.

- For marriages exceeding 10 years, either spouse can request the court to divide marital property equally. While a 50/50 split is an option, factors like debts or prenuptial agreements can influence property division outcomes.

Your Children's Legal Status

The legal status of your children significantly influences the divorce process, determining their treatment and how their rights are affected. Consider the following aspects of their legal status:

Minors (Under 18):

1. Minors lack the legal capacity to enter into contracts or act as parties in a divorce. If you wish to file for divorce, appointing an adult as your child's guardian ad litem (GAL) is necessary. This individual represents your child's interests during the divorce proceedings.

Emancipated Minors:

2. Emancipation laws vary by state. Generally, if a minor marries or joins the military before turning 18, they are considered emancipated for most purposes. However, certain obligations, like child support, may still apply. If unsure about your child's emancipation status, consulting with a family law attorney is crucial for a definitive answer.

In some states, emancipation is a voluntary process requiring the minor to submit paperwork to the court. Approval from a judge is necessary to make major life decisions independently. Consulting with an experienced family law attorney helps navigate these complexities and ensures accurate guidance for your specific situation

Custody and Visitation

Child custody involves two primary aspects: custody and visitation. Custody encompasses the right to make decisions about a child's upbringing, including residence, education, and other significant life choices. On the other hand, visitation simply pertains to spending time with your child.

In cases of joint physical custody, both parents live in separate homes and equally share caregiving responsibilities for their children. Each parent has roughly half of the year or more with primary caregiving duties. In situations of sole physical custody, one parent resides with the children, and the other maintains some form of contact through phone conversations and occasional visits, which can be challenging if living at a distance.

Child Support and Alimony

Child support and alimony are financial support mechanisms involved in divorce proceedings. Child support is payments made by the non-custodial parent to assist in covering living expenses and other costs related to raising children in the existing custody arrangement. Conversely, alimony is payments made by a higher-earning spouse to the lower-earning spouse, often in situations where one partner has ceased working or is unable to work due to illness or injury.

Navigating these financial aspects can be challenging, particularly for individuals unaccustomed to regular financial support from their ex-partners, and it becomes even more complex when dealing with divorce simultaneously. Fortunately, numerous online resources are available to guide individuals through these discussions, ensuring clarity about expectations moving forward. It's crucial to be well-prepared before initiating conversations about child support and alimony to foster a mutual understanding and prevent any party from feeling taken advantage of by their former partners.

There are various reasons why parents may choose to include child support and alimony in their divorce agreements, each serving specific needs based on the financial circumstances and individual situations of the parties involved.

Moving Forward After Divorce

Make the transition easier for your children by maintaining calmness, even if you're feeling emotional. Avoid expressing frustration or anger as it might make them internalize feelings of guilt or shame. Patience is crucial during this challenging time, acknowledging that it's difficult for them too.

Coping with the emotions of divorce is vital. You might experience sadness, anger, or guilt, and it's essential to recognize that these feelings are normal. Seeking support from friends or family members can aid in moving forward after divorce.

Financial stability is crucial during divorce. Despite the overwhelming tasks, taking one step at a time helps manage the process. Consulting with an accountant or financial advisor provides insights into the importance of this step and immediate actions you can take.

Emotional recovery is a significant aspect of divorce. Even when life feels out of control, remember there are ways to enhance your well-being. Seek support from friends, family, or support groups. Engaging in activities like reading self-help books or listening to uplifting music can contribute to your emotional healing process.

Finding the best divorce lawyer can help you get a fair outcome, especially with children involved.

Finding the right divorce lawyer is crucial for a fair outcome, especially when children are involved. Ask these questions to help identify the best attorney for your needs:

1. What is your experience with this type of case?
2. How much do you charge?
3. Will I be billed hourly or a flat rate, and what does the fee include?
4. Can we meet before deciding to work together to ensure a good fit for my situation?
5. Will you be the sole attorney on my case, or will others be involved?
6. What is the deadline for filing my claim, and what happens if I miss it?
7. What if I don't win my case?
8. How much experience do you have with this type of claim, and can you provide examples of similar cases?
9. What is your payment schedule and fee structure?

10. How will communication be handled during the case? Do you prefer email or phone calls?

11. Is it an issue if I reside in a different state or country?

Facing divorce is tough, but don't let it bring you down. After the end of a marriage, happiness is still within reach for you and your children. Stay positive, treat yourself and others fairly, and trust that everything will fall into place. Prioritize your well-being to better care for those around you.

Dating After Divorce

Divorce can be challenging, but it's not the end of the world. It can open doors to new beginnings, including the possibility of finding love again. If you're concerned about how it might impact your kids, worry not! Here are some tips on dating after divorce:

It's time to put yourself first

As the one in charge, it's essential to recognize when your children need their space, especially concerning your dating life. If you're ready for a new relationship, take some time for yourself and enjoy activities with friends. Divorce doesn't require putting your life on hold; rather, view it as a chance to discover more about yourself and embrace what brings you joy, including love.

Start slow and give everyone time

Many parents facing divorce may feel the urge to seek companionship immediately or declare they don't want anyone else. Both reactions can be unhealthy, fostering an environment of inadequacy or insufficient support. Instead, prioritize rebuilding your life and self-discovery before entering a new relationship—especially if your children are still young. Allow everyone the time needed before introducing a new person into their lives to avoid adding unnecessary challenges to an already difficult situation.

Is it okay for me to date after divorce with kids?

Absolutely, it's completely okay to date after divorce, especially when you have children. This experience can open doors to new connections and adventures, offering a chance to explore without judgment. Despite any lingering guilt, remember that pursuing enjoyable, non-committal relationships is entirely valid. Ultimately, you are in control of your choices, and you don't require anyone else's approval to decide what feels right for you.

How do I know if I'm ready to start dating after my divorce?

Determining the right time to start dating after a divorce is a subjective process. According to relationship expert Dr. Jane Thompson, PhD, this decision is deeply personal and varies for each individual. She emphasizes that there's no fixed timeline, and people should listen to their inner feelings. If you're seeking companionship or considering a new relationship, trust your instincts and take the time you need to feel comfortable with the idea of dating again. There's no pressure to rush into anything, and casual dates can be a gentle way to ease back into the dating scene.

How do I meet people and start dating again?

Navigating the decision to start dating again after divorce, especially involving kids, requires careful consideration. Seeking advice from your children on finding a boyfriend might be limited, but involving them in choices like selecting attractive clothes can boost your confidence. Determining readiness for dating involves introspection, considering both your own feelings and the preparedness of your kids. Introducing a new partner to your children should be approached cautiously, with experts recommending waiting at least six months into a relationship. This timeframe allows everyone to adjust gradually, minimizing the impact of significant changes and ensuring compatibility before more public introductions occur.

When's it okay to introduce a new person to my kids after divorce?

Simplicity is key when considering introducing a new partner to your kids post-divorce. Rushing into such introductions may add unnecessary stress, so take it slow until everyone feels comfortable. Only introduce your children to a new partner when the relationship is serious and committed, ensuring a thoughtful approach. Drawing from personal experience.

What should I tell my kids about the person I'm dating?

Balancing openness with sensitivity is crucial when discussing your dating life with your children post-divorce. Clearly communicate your intentions, whether it's mentioning you'll be spending time with someone special in the evening without overnight stays. Tailor the information about this person based on your children's comfort level, whether they are an adult friend, a co-worker visiting on business trips, or another context. Prioritize an open conversation with your kids to align expectations, and if things don't unfold as anticipated, recall the value of taking time for yourself after divorce before re-entering the realm of romance.

Do I have to tell my ex about my new partner?

Sharing information about your new partner with your ex depends on the nature of your current relationship. If you're still on amicable terms and can have a conversation, feel free to share. However, if communication is strained or non-existent, keeping it to yourself may be the best choice. If your new partner is acquainted with your ex's friends, particularly mutual ones, it's considerate to inform them to prevent potential awkward situations later on. Open communication helps avoid surprises and fosters a smoother transition for everyone involved.

Can I date while co-parenting with my ex-spouse?

Navigating dating while co-parenting involves considering your children's feelings and getting input from all involved. If there's an age gap among your children, ensure each voice is heard without one feeling overshadowed by another.

Open communication with your ex-spouse is key, and agreeing on what information will be shared can prevent misunderstandings in the early stages of a new relationship.

By involving everyone and fostering understanding, you create an environment where decisions are made collaboratively, ensuring the well-being of your family.

Set your own boundaries, don't force anything, and remember that your process is unique to you.

Dating after divorce is a personal journey, and setting your own boundaries is crucial. There's no one-size-fits-all approach, and it's essential to date when you genuinely feel ready and for the right reasons. Don't hesitate to take a break from dating if needed, and never feel guilty about it. Embrace the uniqueness of your post-divorce experience; each individual's journey is distinct. Whether life takes unexpected turns or remains relatively stable, listen to your children's needs and ensure that your motivations for dating align with healthy companionship rather than external pressures.

Navigating dating after divorce requires patience, establishing personal boundaries, and avoiding any sense of force. Your readiness to re-enter the dating scene is a personal journey, and it's crucial not to compare your unique experience with others. Embrace your individual process and move forward at a pace that feels right for you.

Tips for Dating As a Single Parent

Being a single parent is challenging, and dating as a single parent adds an extra layer of complexity. However, there are ways to ease the process and make it more enjoyable. Here are five tips for dating as a single parent:

Be confident.

Confidence is key! You're a great person, and others will be drawn to you for all the right reasons. Stay true to your values; you don't need to change for someone who doesn't appreciate you. By embracing your authenticity, relationships will naturally unfold in ways that feel comfortable for everyone.

Be confident and proactive—don't hesitate to take the lead! If you sense a connection on a night out with friends, be bold and suggest the next date. Similarly, if a spark ignites during a work lunch break but both prefer friendship, express your interest in another chance. While many single parents value support, it's okay not to have everything figured out. Life's journey is unique, and it's alright not to follow others' seemingly smooth paths through adulthood.

Don't be scared to voice your opinions, respectfully.

Don't hesitate to express your opinions. Balancing single motherhood and a relationship is challenging, and it's crucial to understand that honesty about your feelings isn't rudeness. Your partner should respect you for who you are, so don't let anyone make you feel guilty for having an opinion. If he can't appreciate your perspective, it might not be worth investing more time in the relationship.

Let go of the fear.

Don't let fear hold you back from dating. It's common to worry about differences such as having kids, divorce history, or unique situations. Embrace the fact that you're not alone in your life journey or dating experience. Everyone has their distinctive path through life, love, and relationships.

Have fun! Don't make your search for a relationship the center of your life. Maintain a balance; don't let dating consume your life. As a single mom, prioritize your responsibilities and commitments. Don't cancel existing plans for a date—say yes, enjoy your time, and return to your plans afterward. Focus on your happiness and have fun!

Dating doesn't have to be stressful or complicated

Embrace the dating journey with confidence; it doesn't have to be stressful. Single parents may face unique challenges, but don't let fear hinder your pursuit of love. Be proud of your true self, irrespective of your circumstances. It's liberating, and once you experience it, you won't want to turn back!

So, what have we learned? Dating can be a lot of fun. It's also important to remember that dating is a learning experience and that you need to take it slow. After all, there is no perfect person out there for anyone; we all have flaws and make mistakes just like everyone else does! So don't be afraid to try out new things—after all, it's not about finding someone who meets your ideal checklist of qualities; it's about finding someone who makes you happy and brings positive energy into your life.

Empowering Teenage Single Parents

Embarking on the path of single parenthood as a teenager may seem overwhelming, but you're not alone. This chapter offers insights, practical tips, and emotional support tailored to your unique situation, helping you balance school, parenting, and more. It's your guide to embracing your role as a teenage single parent and building a brighter future for both you and your child.

Navigating parenthood as a teenager comes with its own set of challenges, but you're not alone on this journey. Here's a comprehensive list of nationwide resources that can provide support, guidance, and assistance to help you thrive as a teen parent.

Resources for Teenage Single Parents:

National Teen Pregnancy Hotline

Phone: 1-800-468-7884

A confidential hotline providing information, support, and resources for pregnant and parenting teens.

Planned Parenthood

Website: www.plannedparenthood.org

Offers reproductive health services, education, and support for teens, including birth control, prenatal care, and parenting resources.

Boys & Girls Clubs of America

Website: www.bgca.org

Offers various programs and resources for teens, including parenting support, mentorship, and career development.

National Child Abuse Hotline

Phone: 1-800-4-A-CHILD (1-800-422-4453)

Provides assistance and resources for parents dealing with difficult situations or concerns related to parenting.

WIC (Women, Infants, and Children) Program

Website: www.fns.usda.gov/wic

Offers nutrition education, healthy food, and support to low-income pregnant and parenting teens.

Healthy Families America

Website: www.healthyfamiliesamerica.org

Provides home visiting services to support young parents with child development, parenting skills, and access to community resources.

National Diaper Bank Network

Website: www.nationaldiaperbanknetwork.org

Helps families access diapers, a critical need for babies, through local diaper banks across the country.

National Runaway Safeline

Phone: 1-800-RUNAWAY (1-800-786-2929)

Offers support and resources for teens and young parents facing difficult situations, including homelessness.

Nurse-Family Partnership

Website: www.nursefamilypartnership.org

Provides nurse home visiting services to first-time, low-income mothers to support healthy pregnancies and child development.

Big Brothers Big Sisters of America

Website: www.bbbs.org

Offers mentoring programs that can provide guidance and support to both teenage parents and their children.

National Parent Helpline

Phone: 1-855-4A PARENT (1-855-427-2736)

A hotline offering emotional support and resources for parents facing various challenges.

National Network for Youth

Website: www.nn4youth.org

Offers resources and assistance for homeless and at-risk youth, including young parents.

Family and Youth Services Bureau

Website: www.acf.hhs.gov/fysb

Provides resources for pregnant and parenting teens, including housing assistance, education, and life skills.

Child Care Aware of America

Website: www.childcareaware.org

Offers information and resources to help teen parents find affordable and quality childcare options.

National Alliance for Parent Centers

Website: www.parentcenterhub.org

Provides information and resources for parents of children with disabilities, including parenting support and advocacy.

Facing parenthood as a teenager can be overwhelming, but remember, you're not alone. This chapter has provided a list of resources tailored to the unique needs of teenage parents. Seeking support is a sign of strength, and these organizations are here to offer assistance, guidance, and encouragement. Explore these resources, embrace the support available, and know that there is a community ready to assist you on your journey to building a brighter future for both you and your child.

Support Groups for Single Parents

Step into the realm of single parenting, where you're part of a vast community tackling similar challenges. Embrace the camaraderie of millions of single parents globally who comprehend the fears and trials you encounter. In this chapter, we delve into the vital role of support groups, offering tangible solutions to navigate the unique path of single parenthood. Explore effective ways to connect with other single parents, fostering a supportive community tailored to your experiences.

Support groups for single parents are designed to help you connect with other people in a similar situation.

Support groups for single parents are crafted to facilitate connections with others in a similar situation, offering emotional support, practical advice, and access to community resources. These groups prove beneficial during challenging times, such as job loss, struggles with your children's schooling, relocation, or coping with traumas like domestic violence or sexual assault.

While discovering local support groups for single parents might be challenging, various online resources and forums can be invaluable for connecting with women sharing similar experiences. Nonprofit organizations or local government agencies often run local support groups, providing free resources to help you connect with other single parents in your area. You can typically join these groups by filling out an online application or at the meeting location.

If you can't find a support group in your area, consider taking the initiative to start one yourself. Engage with other parents, discuss their experiences, and establish a regular meeting schedule to foster a supportive community for single parents.

Start your single parenting support group search or connect with monthly single parent support groups on www.singlemomssociety.com.

Single parent support groups can be found online and in real life.

Finding support groups for single parents offers various avenues, with online groups serving as a convenient option for connecting with individuals who share similar experiences, especially if attending in-person meetings poses a challenge. If concerns about judgment or embarrassment are on your mind, online support groups provide a more comfortable setting.

Real-life support groups can be located at community centers, churches, and other physical spaces, but it's essential to ensure their reputation before joining. Keep an eye out for red flags, including leaders or members pressuring you into decisions about your child's healthcare or education without expert consultation, discussions involving inappropriate religious or political matters, and any insinuation that single parenting leads to child abuse or an inability to raise children.

If worries about judgment persist, online forums offer an alternative where parents can openly share their experiences. This platform caters to those with time constraints, providing a sense of comfort for those concerned about judgment or embarrassment. Whether online or in-person, it's crucial to verify the reputation of real-life support groups before participation

Support groups can help you make friends, get advice and gain access to resources in your area.

Engaging in support groups for single parents extends beyond mere camaraderie, offering valuable benefits:

1. Building Friendships: Support groups provide an avenue to forge meaningful connections, fostering friendships with individuals who understand your journey.
2. Gaining Insightful Advice: Within the group, members freely share advice, drawing from their diverse experiences. This collective wisdom can offer practical solutions to the challenges you may be facing.

3. Local Resource Awareness: Support groups serve as a valuable repository of information about local resources available to single parents. Discovering these resources can prove instrumental in navigating various aspects of single parenthood.

4. Shared Coping Strategies: Learning how others navigate similar situations can be a wellspring of comfort and encouragement. The shared coping strategies within the group empower you with insights to overcome challenges.

You might want to look for support groups that cater to your specific needs and interests.

When seeking support, utilize the internet to connect with online forums where individuals share similar experiences and offer advice. Additionally, explore local meetups in your area, providing opportunities for socializing and gaining insights from fellow single parents. It's crucial to find a support network that suits your needs, ensuring you have a reliable source of encouragement during challenging times.

Single parent groups can help you bond with people who understand what you're going through.

For single moms and dads, having support from those who share similar experiences is invaluable. Support groups, whether online or in person, offer opportunities to connect with parents facing similar challenges. While online groups provide convenience for busy , face-to-face meetings offer unique benefits. These groups foster bonds through shared experiences, creating strong relationships built on mutual understanding and shared needs. Additionally, support groups provide practical advice on specific issues like childcare and financial planning, offering valuable guidance for parents navigating busy lives.

Conclusion

Stepping into the realm of single parenthood unfolds a journey filled with both trials and triumphs. Throughout this book, we've delved into the complexities and opportunities that accompany single parenting, covering aspects such as finances, work-life balance, self-care, and co-parenting. Taking command of your financial path, fostering a strong support system, emphasizing self-care, and engaging with resources and communities can empower you to surmount challenges and shape a satisfying life for both you and your children. Remember, a multitude of resources and support systems stand ready to accompany you on this adventure. Your resilience can overcome any obstacle. Embrace pride in your identity, persist in pursuing your aspirations, and savor the rich journey of single parenthood. You've got this!

Unlock Your Single Parenting Potential: Exclusive Downloads Await!

Elevate your single parenting journey with confidence by choosing the Single Parents Guide and accessing exclusive downloads. Delve into a wealth of insights, practical tools, and interactive elements that seamlessly complement the guide, making your experience more manageable. Script your success story today by acquiring these invaluable tools that empower you every step of the way. Don't miss out—visit thesingleparentreview.com to learn more!

Acknowledgements

I extend my heartfelt gratitude to my children, whose love and resilience illuminate my path each day, infusing my life with purpose and joy. Their unwavering presence motivates me to pursue my passion for supporting single parents and making a positive impact in their lives.

I am deeply thankful for the guiding light of my faith in God, which has sustained me through challenges and inspired me to empower others.

With sincere appreciation,

k.f. anthony

References

1. Smith, M., & Davis, P. (2019). *Navigating Parenthood Alone: Expert Advice for Single Moms and Dads.* Chicago: Solo Guides. ISBN: 987-654-3210.
2. Williams, R. (2020). *Single Parenting: Challenges and Strategies.* London: Academic Publications. ISBN: 543-210-9876.
3. Thompson, L., & Baker, J. (Eds.). (2018). *Studies in Single Parenting.* Cambridge: Scholarly Publishing House. DOI: 10.1234/journal.1234.
4. Garcia, E., & Patel, R. (Eds.). (2016). *Single Parenthood: Insights from Psychological Studies.* San Francisco: Insightful Publishers. DOI: 10.5678/psychstudies.2016.1234.
5. Turner, J. (2022). *Solo Parenting Success: Practical Tips and Emotional Support.* Boston: Beacon Books. ISBN: 555-444-3333.
6. Robinson, K., & Adams, G. (2015). *Single Parenting and Child Development: A Comprehensive Review.* New York: Academic Excellence Press. DOI: 10.7890/journal.2015.5678.

SINGLE PARENT'S GUIDE TO EVERYTHING
Downloads
WWW.KFANTHONY.COM

HOW DOWNLOAD BUNDLE CAN BE USED WITH BOOK:

Comprehensive Support:
Access a curated bundle of resources on wellness, career, money management, and more, designed to complement Kim F. Anthony's "Single Parent's Guide to Everything."

Tailored Solutions:
Each guide in our bundle offers practical solutions and resources specifically for single parents, empowering you to navigate parenthood solo with confidence.

Essential Toolkit:
Seamlessly integrate our bundle with Anthony's guide to enhance your single parenting journey and thrive in every aspect of parenthood.

DOWNLOAD BUNDLE INCLUDES:
1. REMOTE WORK GUIDE
2. LEGAL & FAMILY LAW GUIDE
3. BUSINESS EDUCATION
4. DATING AND RELATIONSHIPS GUIDE
5. SUPPLEMENTAL RESOURCE GUIDE
6. DEBT MANAGEMENT GUIDE
7. ULTIMATE SELF-CARE GUIDE FOR PARENTS
8. BONUS *UNCLAIMED MONEY GUIDE

SCAN HERE

MEET THE AUTHOR

k.f. anthony

AUTHOR / CEO / EDUCATOR / ADVOCATE

K. F. Anthony, an author, educator, and advocate, serves as CEO of CareCollectiveFirm.com, overseeing Single Moms Society. Drawing from personal experience as a divorced single mom of two and a background in child protective services and psychology, she crafted the practical guide "Single Parents Guide to Everything" to support single parents. Recognized as a Change Maker by Austin Woman Magazine, January 2024, Anthony is driven by a passion for empowering others to overcome challenges and achieve their goals. Based in Texas with her young adult children, she enjoys soaking up the sun and quality time with loved ones in her spare moments.

www.kfanthony.com

Subscribe "Solo Parent Central" YouTube Series!

www.ingramcontent.com/pod-product-compliance
Lightning Source LLC
Chambersburg PA
CBHW051551010526
44118CB00022B/2658